# THE EMOTION BEHIND MONEY WORKBOOK

# THE EMOTION BEHIND MONEY WORKBOOK

BUILDING WEALTH *from the* INSIDE OUT

JULIE MARIE MURPHY, CFP®

Beyond Your Wildest Dreams, LLC
Chicago, Illinois

**Beyond Your Wildest Dreams, LLC**
**1017 W Washington Blvd**
**Chicago, IL 60607**

ISBN 978-0-578-83762-8

An application to register this book for cataloging
has been submitted to the Library of Congress.

Book design by BYJ Communications, Inc.
Cover design by MACook Design

PLEASE NOTE: The views, comments, and opinions expressed within this writing are solely those of Julie Murphy, not those of any co-workers, managers, broker-dealer staff or management, regulators, or other industry professionals except where specifically cited. The ideas and opinions presented are not meant to fit every individual and in some cases, professional help in the form of medical, tax, and legal advice may be necessary and should be obtained from qualified professionals before attempting to implement serious changes to your life.

The hypothetical illustrations contained herein are intended solely to depict how a Financial Advisor may obtain and implement recommendations suited to an individual or business need. The depictions in these examples have been created from a compilation of clients, are for illustrative purposes only, and do not reflect the actual performance of any particular investment or the analysis of the needs of an actual person or business. For more information about the options available, please contact a qualified professional. Julie Murphy does not offer tax advice. The tax information contained herein is general and is not exhaustive by nature. It was not intended or written to be used, and it cannot be used by any taxpayer for the purpose of avoiding penalties that may be imposed on the taxpayer under U.S. federal tax laws. Federal and state tax laws are complex and constantly changing. You should always consult your own legal or tax advisor for information concerning your individual situation.

This material is neither an offer to sell nor the solicitation of an offer to buy any security, which can only be made by the prospectus which has been filed or registered with the appropriate state and federal agencies, and sold only by broker/dealers authorized to do so. No regulatory agency has passed on or endorsed the merit of this material. Any representation to the contrary is un-lawful. All trademarks referenced herein are the property of their respective owners.

# CONTENTS

# ACKNOWLEDGEMENTS

Heartfelt thanks to Karyn Pettigrew; Linda McCabe; my son, Timmy; Jean Chatzky; Carmen Wong Ulrich; Alexis Martin Neely; Jeff Cox; Anne Emerson; Tarra in Se-dona; Bob Lyman; Mark Murphy; Jeff Ragan; Meeghan Holly; Veronica Erxleben; Melissa Casserly; Becky Murphy; Vanessa Sheehan; Candy Mayer; Rachel Lukawski; Athena Golianis; Chris Deschaine; MaryBeth Wilke; Jim Courtright; Lori Keenan; Dr. Sandy Goldberg; Donna Gutman; Heidi Bell; Carolyn Chmiel; Sheila Shaughnessy; Janet Powers; Mary Ann Daly; Jen Medina Ragan; Travis McKay; and my many clients, friends and colleagues. Last but not least, thanks to my feng shui hair designers, Paula Miyashiro and Maria Romero, for making me camera ready.

I would also like to thank the following organizations, which have supported my mission to financially heal our world: CNBC, NBC, The Chopra Center, Pacific Life Insurance Company, Wells Real Estate, LPL Financial, Woman of the World, Holistic Moms, the National Association of Financial Advisors, Chicago Healers, CNL Real Estate, Fidelity, Sun Life Insurance Company, Partners Publishers Group, Mishka Productions, Shakespeare Squared, Extraordinary Outcomes and Oprah Radio.

Thank you all for offering your talents, time and energy to help make my dreams become a reality!

# INTRODUCTION

Are you tired of feeling as if your finances control your life? Are you ready to make peace with money once and for all? In the eight years since I started my wealth management practice, I've guided thousands of people through the process of financial healing. I can tell you without reservation that healing your relationship with money will illuminate the path to financial abundance and inner peace. By reading my book *The Emotion Behind Money: Building Wealth from the Inside Out* and completing the exercises in this workbook, you will finally process the emotions you associate with money and discover how to create harmony and balance in every aspect of your life.

My book and this workbook guide you through each step of the process toward financial health. The first step is to unplug from the outside world and focus inward, on your authentic self and the Inner Wealth you naturally possess. The second step is to define your dreams, desires and passions, so that you know what you really want out of life. Finally, you must create a Personal Navigation Route. This plan will get you from where you are to where you want to go. And I'll be with you every step of the way.

Before we begin, I encourage you to acknowledge your inner critic—you know, the little voice that insists your dreams are silly and your emotions unwarranted. As you read *The Emotion Behind Money* and complete the pages in this workbook, your inner critic is bound to pop up from time to time, insisting that you're incapable of solving your money problems. Make a habit of countering any critical thoughts you might have with supportive statements, such as, "Wow, I've spent so many years feeling this way. No wonder money issues are so painful for me," or "I'm choosing to think about this issue in a new way this time." Positive thoughts like these help heal the emotional wounds that prevent us from living the lives we really want.

The exercises in this workbook move chronologically through my book *The Emotion Behind Money*. Some of the workbook pages correspond directly with exercises in the book and give you the space and the support you need to complete them. The workbook also contains many additional exercises not found in the book.

It's time now to take your first steps toward discovering your authentic life. It's an exciting time to be you!

Wishing you a passionate and purposeful life,

Julie Murphy

# SECTION ONE
## The Big Picture

# YOUR INNER WEALTH

*"When I chased after money, I never had enough. When I got my life on purpose and focused on giving of myself and everything that arrived into my life, then I was prosperous."*

—Wayne Dyer

# TAKING STOCK

Does it surprise you to know that your financial health depends on more than your accumulation of literal wealth? Let's step back and consider the big picture. First we'll take stock of the emotions, attitudes and beliefs you have about money.

Choose the sentences below that most accurately describe you. Be as authentic as you can. Just recognize exactly where you are.

## ATTITUDE INVENTORY

☐ I worry about money, no matter how much or how little I have.

☑ I dream about being financially secure.

☐ The main reason I work is so I can buy the things I want.

☐ My anxiety about or preoccupation with money affects my physical health, my time with my family or other aspects of my life.

☑ If I just had enough money, I would be happy. *think it sometimes but know its not true*

☑ My financial well-being is out of my control.

☑ I make poor financial choices—small and large—that I later regret.

☐ Whether or not I reach my life goals depends on how much money I have.

☐ I feel empowered and energetic about my finances.

☐ I feel financially secure or on the road to financial security.

☐ I do work that satisfies my sense of purpose in the world.

☐ The financial realm of my life is in balance with the other aspects of my life.

☐ I feel happy and satisfied with my life.

☐ My financial well-being is determined by my attitude toward money and the financial choices I make.

☐ When I feel insecure about money, I don't make any major financial decisions without consulting a trusted advisor.

☐ I am confident that I will reach my life goals regardless of the surrounding circumstances.

# THE LIFE NAVIGATION WHEEL

Now that you've acknowledged some of your core beliefs about money, let's explore how your finances affect the other aspects of your life by completing the Life Navigation Wheel. The wheel illustrates how we prioritize the five realms of our lives. One of these realms is at the center of your wheel. It's the motivation behind practically every decision you make. It creates a powerful force, a gravitational pull that keeps all other aspects of your life circling it in an emotional and spiritual orbit.

Fill in the blank wheel below to show the relationship between the five realms in your life. Complete the diagram so that it represents your life at the present time. Be as realistic and honest as you can.

## THE FIVE REALMS

- Financial Life (money, possessions, investments)
- Personal Life (interests, hobbies, friendships, self-improvement)
- Family Life (spouse, children, parents, siblings, home life)
- Work Life (work, continuing education, professional development)
- Spiritual Life (which I refer to as Life Purpose/Inner Wealth; conscience, values, core beliefs)

## LIFE NAVIGATION WHEEL

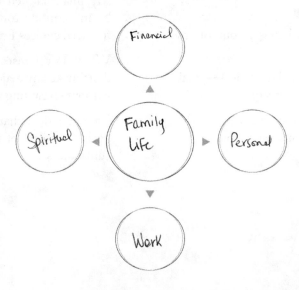

I'm astounded by the shame, guilt, sadness and regret my clients often feel when identifying what is at the center of their lives. I believe these feelings surface when deep within us there is a conflict between what we think our life's focus *should* be and what it actually is.

**Process It** Take a few moments here to deepen your understanding of your emotional reaction.

 Which realm of life did you write in the center of your Life Navigation Wheel?

 *Family*

 Describe how this realm affects the other realms of your life. Do you fear losing your job because you need the money to maintain a certain standard of living? Do you spend a lot of your current cash flow to pay off debt from past choices? Do you spend time working that you would rather spend with your family? Do you have a dream that you've been putting off because you're convinced you simply don't have time to make it a reality?

*My family supercedes all other areas. I do make bad choices sometimes that lead to debt. I do have dreams that are on hold till daughter is through college.*

**Reflect On It** If you're like I was, or even remotely similar to the thousands of people I've counseled over the years, the center of your life is either financial or professional. American culture encourages us to place money at the center of everything. Sadly, money does not bring happiness. You never hear of a person on her deathbed saying, "I wish I had worked more and had more money."

At a pivotal point in my own development, I turned my focus away from money and let my Inner Wealth lead the way. Your Inner Wealth is the part of you that contains all of the nonphysical characteristics that make up your spiritual DNA. It's also the source of your dreams, your desires, your individuality and your life's purpose.

 Imagine the specific ways in which your life would change if you placed your Life Purpose/Inner Wealth at the center of your wheel.

*I would get a college degree + probably change jobs. I'd possibly foster children in need.*

# YOUR INNER WEALTH

*The Emotion Behind Money* **Exercise 1**

Now let's focus on the details of your Inner Wealth. The components of Inner Wealth include your priorities (what's important to you), your values and your core beliefs. List these things in the chart below, in no particular order. Remember, it's about just recognizing where you are today, removing all shame, blame and judgments. I know it's tough, but you can do it! The key here is to make sure to put down the first thing that comes to you before filtering it out. Don't wonder why and if you should put it down—just do it. It will all come together.

| INNER WEALTH | |
|---|---|
| **My Priorities: What's Important to Me** (e.g., my spouse, kids, siblings, parents, job title, service to others, money in the bank) | |
| **My Values** (e.g., honesty, courage, loyalty, responsibility, integrity, frugality) | |
| **My Core Beliefs** (in a higher power, in hard work, in taking care of family, in financial stability, in community involvement, in freedom of expression) | |

**Process It** Did you have a strong emotional reaction as you filled out the chart? Was your reaction different from what you expected? Acknowledge and explore your feelings by considering these questions:

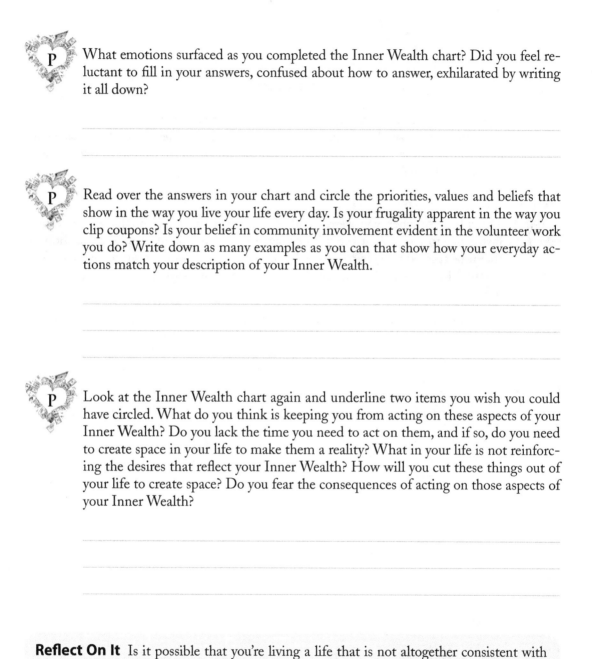

**P**   What emotions surfaced as you completed the Inner Wealth chart? Did you feel reluctant to fill in your answers, confused about how to answer, exhilarated by writing it all down?

_____

_____

**P**   Read over the answers in your chart and circle the priorities, values and beliefs that show in the way you live your life every day. Is your frugality apparent in the way you clip coupons? Is your belief in community involvement evident in the volunteer work you do? Write down as many examples as you can that show how your everyday actions match your description of your Inner Wealth.

_____

_____

_____

**P**   Look at the Inner Wealth chart again and underline two items you wish you could have circled. What do you think is keeping you from acting on these aspects of your Inner Wealth? Do you lack the time you need to act on them, and if so, do you need to create space in your life to make them a reality? What in your life is not reinforcing the desires that reflect your Inner Wealth? How will you cut these things out of your life to create space? Do you fear the consequences of acting on those aspects of your Inner Wealth?

_____

_____

_____

**Reflect On It**   Is it possible that you're living a life that is not altogether consistent with your priorities, values and beliefs? If so, welcome to the human race, my friend. Recognizing this gap between thought and action is the first step in the financial healing process.

# IN SEARCH OF YOUR
# AUTHENTIC SELF
*EBM* Exercise 2

As I had to teach myself to do, you must learn to direct your attention away from money and toward the priorities, values and beliefs that you listed in your Inner Wealth chart. We each have an emotional and spiritual infrastructure that guides us through life. This infrastructure is who you are—your authentic self.

 Think back to when you were a child. Can you recall doing anything that seemed instinctive to you? What activities engaged you to the point of total absorption, so that time seemed to fly by? Did you build a mean sand castle or put on plays for your parents? In the space below, list, describe or draw the activities that came naturally to you.

**Process It** You most likely have pulled up joyous memories. Give yourself a few moments to let that joy sink in.

List your gifts and talents that were apparent in the activities you loved as a child.

_____

_____

Which of these gifts and talents have you nurtured in your adult life? If you haven't used these gifts in your adult life, how could you use them now? If you could do any-thing, the thing that you can do better than anyone else, what would that be?

_____

_____

_____

What or whom has blocked you from nurturing your gifts as an adult?

_____

_____

_____

**Reflect On It** Kids are experts at expressing their Inner Wealth in their everyday actions because they haven't yet learned to doubt or judge themselves and their dreams. Children have no filter!

When we hear the word *childish*, we think "immature" or "juvenile," but when we hear *childlike*, we think "innocent" or "uncomplicated." In what ways might you allow yourself to be more childlike? What can you do to live more in the present moment of your life?

# IN SEARCH OF YOUR
# AUTHENTIC SELF
*(continued)*

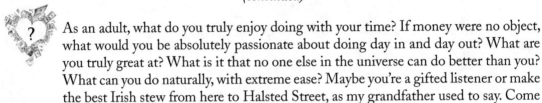 As an adult, what do you truly enjoy doing with your time? If money were no object, what would you be absolutely passionate about doing day in and day out? What are you truly great at? What is it that no one else in the universe can do better than you? What can you do naturally, with extreme ease? Maybe you're a gifted listener or make the best Irish stew from here to Halsted Street, as my grandfather used to say. Come on, don't be modest. List, describe or draw your answers in the space below.

**Process It** Congratulations! I expect that you learned something about yourself that you hadn't really thought of before. Now take a few moments to deepen your awareness about what you've written. Sink into that place deep inside you and recognize how you feel at the very core of your being.

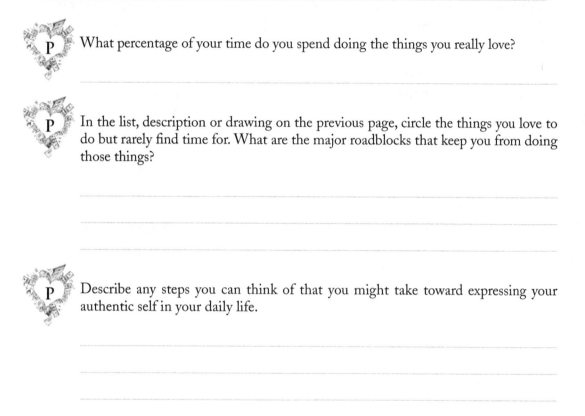

What percentage of your time do you spend doing the things you really love?

In the list, description or drawing on the previous page, circle the things you love to do but rarely find time for. What are the major roadblocks that keep you from doing those things?

Describe any steps you can think of that you might take toward expressing your authentic self in your daily life.

**Reflect On It** If you know who you are and what you want your life to be, and you express your identity and intentions through practical action, the money will follow. Many feel that this approach is counterintuitive, but trust me, this is how it works!

Set an intention about expressing your authentic self in your everyday life. Think of one simple act that will reinforce that intention, and do it! Then bask in the feeling of supreme satisfaction you will get from following up an intention with an action. I'll even give you permission to pat yourself on the back. You're on the road to aligning your life with your authentic self. Isn't this great? Hang on, here we go!

# GETTING WHAT YOU WANT
*EBM* **Exercise 3**

We all have patterns of behavior—some healthy, some less so—that get us things in life. Some behaviors get us what we want, while others bring about less-desirable effects. Let's identify and analyze the patterns in your behavior that have gotten you where you are today.

With an understanding that there are lessons embedded in all life experiences, describe a recent disappointment, missed opportunity or regret.

_____

_____

_____

What caused this less-than-desirable outcome? Describe what happened.

_____

_____

_____

_____

Whom do you feel was responsible for this outcome? Why do you think you feel that way?

_____

_____

_____

_____

Being as honest and authentic as you can, check all the answers that apply to your situation.

The situation began when

- ☐ I set a goal.
- ☐ someone asked me to do something.
- ☐ I asked someone to do something for me.
- ☐ other _____.

The trouble began when I

- ☐ expected something that didn't happen.
- ☐ agreed to do something I didn't want to do.
- ☐ depended upon the wrong person.
- ☐ other _____.

In dealing with the other people involved in the process, my demeanor was

- ☐ charming.
- ☐ businesslike.
- ☐ demanding.
- ☐ passive.
- ☐ other _____.

When things didn't work out, I felt

- ☐ embarrassed.
- ☐ guilty or ashamed.
- ☐ accepting or grateful that I had learned something.
- ☐ furious.
- ☐ other _____.

When things didn't work out, I

- ☐ expressed regret to those involved.
- ☐ expressed anger at those involved.
- ☐ held a debriefing with those involved.
- ☐ ignored the results and moved on.
- ☐ decided to do things differently next time.
- ☐ other _____.

My reaction in this situation was typical.

☐ Yes ☐ No

**Reflect On It** Ask yourself in the most loving way possible if the behaviors you engaged in and the emotions you experienced during this transaction were healthy or harmful. Is it possible that you are taking either too little or too much responsibility for what happened?

# GETTING WHAT YOU WANT
*(continued)*

Now that you've examined a less-than-ideal situation, let's take a look at the bright side!

**?** Describe a recent success, achievement or acquisition.

_____

_____

_____

**?** What steps did you take to get what you wanted?

_____

_____

_____

_____

**?** Whom do you feel was responsible for the outcome of this situation? Explain why you think you feel that way.

_____

_____

_____

_____

Being as honest and authentic as you can, check all the answers that apply to your situation.

The process of getting what I wanted was

- ☐ not as difficult as I thought it would be.
- ☐ more difficult than I thought it would be.
- ☐ not more or less difficult than I expected.
- ☐ other _____.

During the process, I felt

- ☐ anxious.
- ☐ relaxed.
- ☐ angry.
- ☐ determined.
- ☐ other _____.

In dealing with the other people involved in the process, my demeanor was

- ☐ charming.
- ☐ businesslike.
- ☐ demanding.
- ☐ passive.
- ☐ other _____.

In order to get what I wanted, I felt I had to

- ☐ be straightforward and firm.
- ☐ play the victim to gain someone's sympathy.
- ☐ explore multiple avenues before reaching my goal.
- ☐ move too quickly for fear of losing out on what I wanted.
- ☐ bully someone.
- ☐ tell some white lies.
- ☐ do a lot of research first.
- ☐ other _____.

Once I had met my goal, I felt

- ☐ proud.
- ☐ guilty or ashamed.
- ☐ disappointed.
- ☐ satisfied.
- ☐ other _____.

I usually get what I want.

☐ Yes ☐ No

**Reflect On It** Ask yourself in a heartfelt way if the behaviors you engaged in and the emotions you experienced during this transaction were healthy or harmful. Your answers are neither right nor wrong. They are just part of identifying your patterns of behavior.

# GETTING WHAT YOU WANT
*(continued)*

You probably have a clearer picture now of the methods you use to get what you want. Let's take some time to draw some broader conclusions about how certain behaviors have affected your life.

In the left column of the chart on the opposite page, make a list of what you love about your life. Think about how you acquired or achieved those things. Then, in the second column, try to identify the specific behaviors—for example, hard work, courage, patience—that helped you.

**Reflect On It** We all fall back on less-desirable behaviors at times to get what we want. It is only by becoming aware of the downside of such behaviors that we have a chance to change them. Look at the answers you wrote in the chart and think of one specific way you might change a behavior that you feel is undesirable. If you usually manage your employees through intimidation, for example, you might decide to find out what motivates your employees by creating an employee survey.

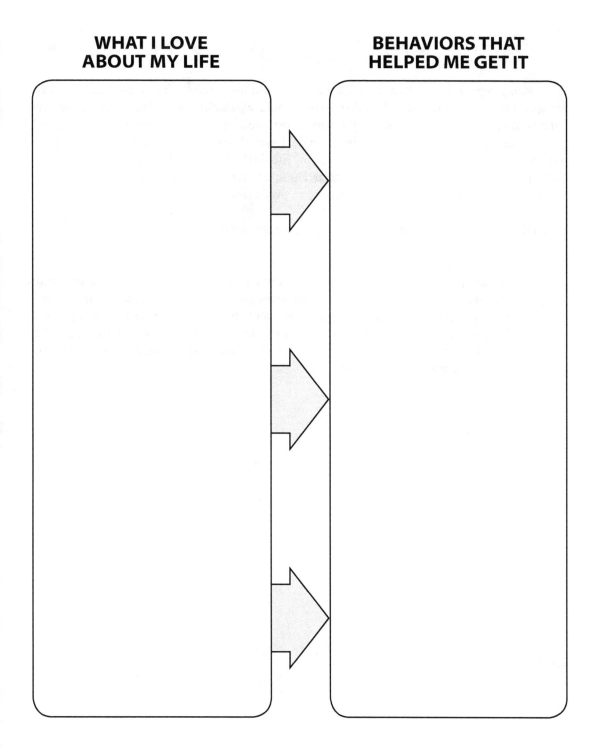

**WHAT I LOVE ABOUT MY LIFE**

**BEHAVIORS THAT HELPED ME GET IT**

# YOUR INHERITED MONEY PATTERNS

At a young age, I found that I had a talent for earning money, but I also had a talent for spending it. As an adult, I realized that I had a scarcity mentality, modeled on my parents' money pattern. Considering I had eleven siblings, it's no surprise that I learned growing up that there would never be enough. I was shocked, however, to realize that my money pattern had leaked into other areas of my life, including my behavior toward food. As a child, I would immediately devour any treat I got, for fear that if I didn't, I would lose it. As an adult, I discovered that this pattern led to overeating.

Let's take a closer look at your inherited money pattern and the emotions that drive it.

In the space below, describe the role money played in your family while you were growing up. Was there a scarcity or an abundance of money at home and in the surrounding community? Did your parents openly talk about money? Did your parents fight or complain about money? When money was discussed, was it stressful? Did your parents use money to make up for not being with you much as a child? Was money the main focal point of life?

Compare your personal relationship with money as a child and as an adult. How did you feel about money then? How do you feel about it now? In what specific ways have you duplicated your parents' money pattern?

_____

_____

_____

_____

_____

Describe at least one way your money pattern has affected your behavior in other areas of your life. Do you find yourself overspending and overeating, as I did? Does your procrastination in relation to paying bills and balancing your checkbook leak over into the way you deal with work assignments or returning phone calls? Is your hoarding attitude toward money also reflected in a sometimes ungenerous attitude toward friends and family? Answer as honestly and with as much self-acceptance as you can.

_____

_____

_____

_____

_____

_____

**Reflect On It**  Think about the relationships in your life—relationships with your parents, your siblings, your spouse, your children, your friends, your co-workers. In what ways does your money pattern affect these connections and vice versa?

# TOXIC EMOTIONS
## *EBM* Exercise 4

David Simon, M.D., co-founder of the Chopra Center for Wellbeing, estimates that over 90 percent of the toxins in the human body develop from toxic emotions—emotions that we ignore or repress and therefore do not process effectively. I've found that some of these repressed emotions are manifested in our relationships with money.

 Which of the feelings below do you associate with money? Circle as many as you feel apply to you. In the space at the bottom of the box, add any other emotions that seem appropriate to you.

| | | | | |
|---|---|---|---|---|
| confidence | powerlessness | happiness | anxiety | resentment |
| dependence | peace | fear | gratitude | anger |
| confusion | despair | freedom | avoidance | joy |
| frustration | jealousy | irritation | ignorance | guilt |

**Reflect On It** Feelings are neither right nor wrong—they just are. But when you continually ignore the messages your emotions are sending you, they will keep coming at you, with increasing severity, year after year, like an emotional two-by-four that keeps cracking you over the head until you truly listen. Ouch! Why do we do this to ourselves? Life is not supposed to be a constant struggle. The good news is that we can change at any point in our lives. It's our choice! Which route will you choose?

**Process It** Getting in touch with your toxic emotions is as easy as the children's rule for crossing the street: Stop, Look and Listen.

## STOP:

Did you wake up Monday morning feeling a little blue? Is it all you can do to drag yourself out of bed? Stop and take a breath. Allow yourself to think about what might actually be bothering you, whether it's kids' soccer schedules or next week's quarterly meeting. Write down some of the things you're worried about right now.

_____

_____

_____

_____

_____

## LOOK:

When you get in the car to drive to work, look at your hands on the steering wheel and your eyes in the rearview mirror. Are your knuckles white from clenching the wheel? Are your eyes narrowed in ire? Describe the physical manifestations of toxic emotions that you see and feel in your body right now.

_____

_____

_____

_____

_____

# TOXIC EMOTIONS
*(continued)*

## LISTEN:

On your way to work, instead of switching on the radio or plugging in to your MP3 player, listen to the silence. Try to shut out the busy chatter in your head and focus on your emotions. Being as accepting as you can, recognize whatever feelings come to the surface, the sadness or frustration that shows itself as anger, rage, jealousy or envy. How are you feeling right now?

# YOUR INNER WEALTH:
# TYING IT ALL TOGETHER

When you put your Inner Wealth at the center of your life and let it direct your every decision, you can then live a more harmonic life. Uneasy feelings come when your life is not in harmony with your soul's purpose. They're the language spoken by your subconscious in an effort to communicate with your conscious mind. Whenever I get one of those pesky feelings, I understand that my emotions are trying to tell me that something is not aligned between my Life's Purpose and my actions—that is, between my inner world and my external world.

Take the first step toward aligning your Life's Purpose and your actions by setting your inten-tions in the chart below.

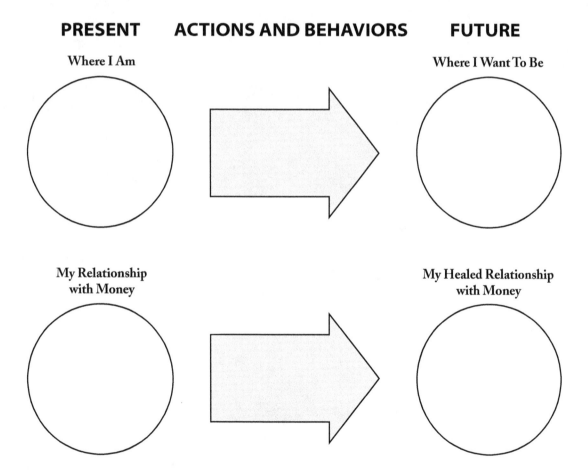

| PRESENT | ACTIONS AND BEHAVIORS | FUTURE |
|---|---|---|
| Where I Am | | Where I Want To Be |
| My Relationship with Money | | My Healed Relationship with Money |

# THE SEARCH FOR HAPPINESS

*"The purpose of our lives is to be happy."*

—Dalai Lama

# ACQUISITION EXERCISE
## *The Emotion Behind Money* Exercise 5

Visualize the last time you bought yourself something that brought you satisfaction—something that, in the moment, excited you. Later, however, when the credit card bill came in, you experienced a spending hangover. You felt sweaty, queasy or sick to your stomach. Once you had to pay for that financial decision, you found yourself stressed or even filled with dread. We've all been there! Many of us have this experience in January, after the holiday spending spree. Now, dig down in your heart to answer the questions below.

What was the item in question?

_____

Did you buy this item to make yourself feel happy?

☐ Yes  ☐ No

Did you buy this item to appease or make someone else happy?

☐ Yes  ☐ No

If yes, whom?

_____

Did you buy it because you were tired of doing without and just said, "What the heck, I'm going to do it"?

☐ Yes  ☐ No

If you bought it to make someone else happy, were you trying to buy his or her love? (Many parents today feel guilty because they want to spend more time with their kids, but they also both need to work, so they buy them things out of guilt.)

☐ Yes  ☐ No

Did you buy this item to feel accepted in your community or neighborhood?

☐ Yes  ☐ No

If yes, why do you want to be accepted by this group?

_____

_____

_____

Is the item really something that you wanted?  ☐ Yes  ☐ No

Do you fear that without it you won't fit in?  ☐ Yes  ☐ No

Are you an emotional spender, meaning do you buy when you're happy or sad?

☐ Yes  ☐ No

Did your purchase bring you closer to your dreams and desires or move you farther away?

_____

# ACQUISITION EXERCISE

*(continued)*

Did you make this purchase without really internalizing what impact it would have on you and your household?

☐ Yes  ☐ No

What emotions did you temporarily numb or satisfy when you made this purchase?

_____

_____

_____

**Reflect On It** Most overspending occurs because we are trying to solve a deeper problem. We want relief from inner pain or discomfort, but rarely does a new acquisition make the unsettling feelings go away permanently. Recognizing the financial chaos you create through emotional spending is the first step toward realizing your dreams and desires.

# THE MIND/BODY CONNECTION

Some Eastern philosophies teach that the human body consists of seven major zones of energy, regulated through the seven major chakras. According to these belief systems, enlightenment comes from allowing energy to flow freely through the chakras. I believe that toxic emotions can clog the chakras that process emotion, and thus cause illness and disease.

In her book *Anatomy of the Spirit,* Caroline Myss describes a woman who emotionally buries the conflicts in her relationships. Someone like this, Myss states, typically develops breast cancer in her later years. The example reminded me vividly of my mom, who has had a double mastectomy. Along the same lines, half of all my male clients between the ages of 55 and 65 have some type of problem in the area of their hips or lower intestines. As I dug deeper, I discovered that these problems eventually developed into prostate, liver or colon cancer.

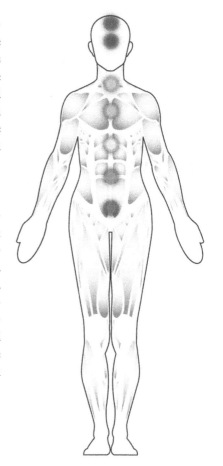

According to Deepak Chopra, a cancer cell develops because that cell has lost its sense of purpose. Many of these male clients of mine have defined themselves for years as the providers of their households. Now the children are grown, their wives are no longer dependent on them, and in many cases, their employers are replacing them with younger, less expensive employees. I believe that these men's emotional toxins have clogged the energy flow in their lower chakras.

 Look at the illustration of the chakras and mentally locate each chakra on your own body. Then take a few moments to breathe deeply. Visualize breathing through each one of your chakras. Imagine that your chakras are clear and open. Now close your eyes and try to identify the places on your body that feel tense or tender or painful, especially in areas close to the first, second and third chakras on your lower body. Imagine each exhalation of breath carrying away any pain or tension from your body.

# HAPPINESS EXERCISE
## *EBM* Exercise 6

Finding happiness begins with recognizing your participation in your own life and taking responsibility for your own happiness. Answer the following questions, accepting any emotions that might be stirred up along the way. Write down your thoughts just as they come.

Sit quietly and ask yourself, "Am I happy?" If not, why not? Do you want to be happy? Do you believe that you can have happiness or that you deserve happiness?

What if you sought healing from Dr. Chopra and he asked you why you want to live? What would you say? What do you live for?

Close your eyes and think back to a time in your life when you were truly happy. Re-live the joy you felt. Feel it tickling your heart. What was happening in your life at the time? What was the source of your joy?

_____

_____

_____

_____

_____

What can you do in your life now to recreate that period or moment of bliss?

_____

_____

_____

_____

_____

# HARMONY EXERCISE
### *EBM* Exercise 7

I believe that inner healing leads to outward health, and I believe bringing peace to your inner emotions is the place where healing begins. I invite and encourage you to embrace the concept of inner peace and harmony with all your heart. Harmony means being in the right relationship with your authentic self. Let your authentic self shine out to the world, and the money will follow.

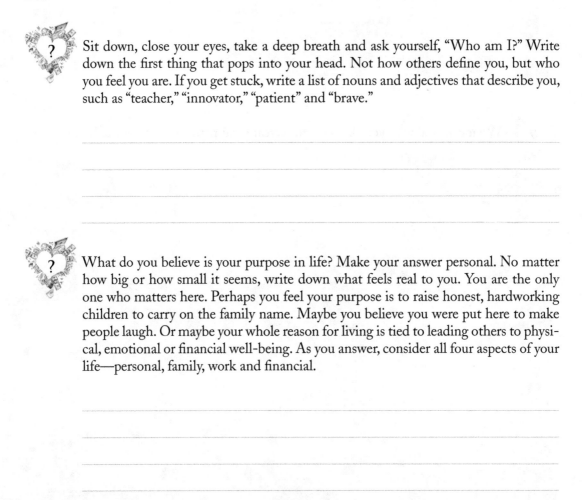

Sit down, close your eyes, take a deep breath and ask yourself, "Who am I?" Write down the first thing that pops into your head. Not how others define you, but who you feel you are. If you get stuck, write a list of nouns and adjectives that describe you, such as "teacher," "innovator," "patient" and "brave."

_____

_____

_____

_____

What do you believe is your purpose in life? Make your answer personal. No matter how big or how small it seems, write down what feels real to you. You are the only one who matters here. Perhaps you feel your purpose is to raise honest, hardworking children to carry on the family name. Maybe you believe you were put here to make people laugh. Or maybe your whole reason for living is tied to leading others to physical, emotional or financial well-being. As you answer, consider all four aspects of your life—personal, family, work and financial.

_____

_____

_____

_____

Now, let's see if your sense of self and your life's purpose are in harmony with what happens in the harsh daylight of everyday life. In the circles below, describe your current reality, good and bad, as it applies to each area. For example, in your Work Life circle, you might write, "I don't enjoy my job." Write down the specifics as well, such as "I travel too much" or "My company is unethical."

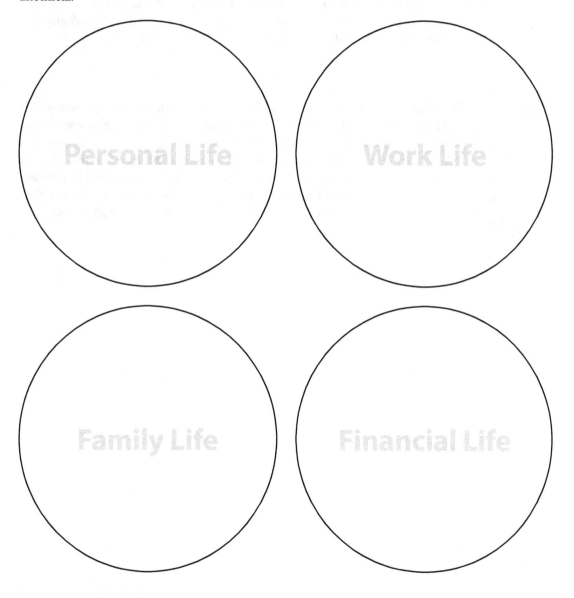

# HARMONY EXERCISE
### (continued)

**Process It** Compare the statements you wrote in the circles to the words you used to describe yourself and your life's purpose. For example, maybe you described yourself as outgoing and fun, but in your Personal Life circle, you wrote down that you don't get asked out on many dates. Or maybe one of the adjectives you chose to describe yourself was "passionate," yet in your Work Life circle you wrote that you're bored to tears in your uncreative job.

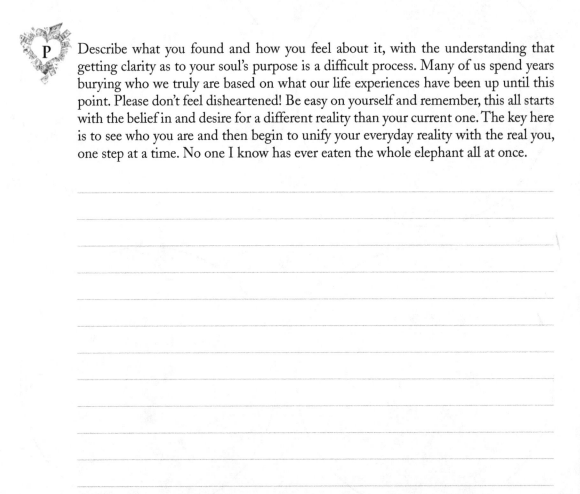 Describe what you found and how you feel about it, with the understanding that getting clarity as to your soul's purpose is a difficult process. Many of us spend years burying who we truly are based on what our life experiences have been up until this point. Please don't feel disheartened! Be easy on yourself and remember, this all starts with the belief in and desire for a different reality than your current one. The key here is to see who you are and then begin to unify your everyday reality with the real you, one step at a time. No one I know has ever eaten the whole elephant all at once.

# THE SEARCH FOR HAPPINESS:
# TYING IT ALL TOGETHER

Western culture has us believing that "things" and "stuff" bring happiness. As a result, many of us today live in a cycle of constant struggle to earn more to get more. It's as if we are all chasing our tails. In the meantime our quality of life suffers. Much of this suffering is because we use the money we get today to pay for all of our past choices by paying down debt. If we are always spending today's money on yesterday, how can we ever live in the present moment, let alone plan for what we want in our futures? It's as if we've become caged animals and we can't break free. Financial responsibility is not a principle that our society upholds, resulting in a lower savings rate in America than during the Great Depression.

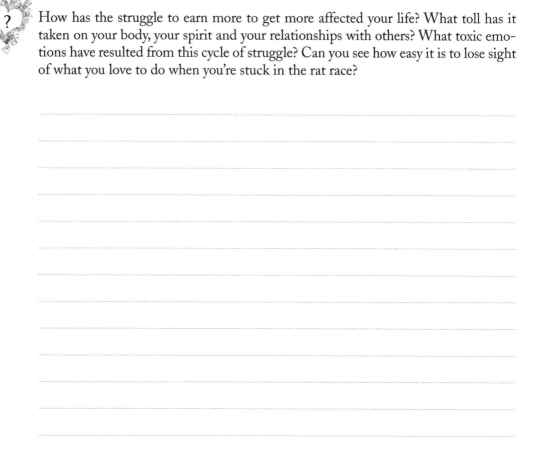

How has the struggle to earn more to get more affected your life? What toll has it taken on your body, your spirit and your relationships with others? What toxic emotions have resulted from this cycle of struggle? Can you see how easy it is to lose sight of what you love to do when you're stuck in the rat race?

# THE SEARCH FOR HAPPINESS:
# TYING IT ALL TOGETHER
*(continued)*

You will remain trapped in a cycle of want until two things occur: one, you discover what truly makes you happy, your deepest dreams and desires; and two, you learn to live your everyday life in harmony with your authentic self.

How have you used money to try to buy happiness? What do you truly think will make you happy?

_____

_____

_____

_____

_____

Describe two specific ways you intend to express your authentic self in your everyday life. It's all right to start small. The key here is to meet yourself exactly where you are and to understand exactly what you are comfortable doing today. You can broaden your horizons as time goes on.

_____

_____

_____

_____

_____

3

# BREAKING AWAY FROM INHERITED BELIEFS

*"Choose beliefs that serve your soul—
choose beliefs that serve the grander
dream of who you choose to be."*

—Joy Page

# YOUR FINANCIAL UPBRINGING
### *The Emotion Behind Money* Exercise 8

Childhood may be short, but its effects last a lifetime. Your parents or caregivers were sending you a money vibe long before you even thought about opening a checking account, and their influence on you, productive or counterproductive, kept working long after you left home. As honestly as you can, answer the questions here to help identify the tribal comforts and beliefs that might be roadblocks in your journey to financial health.

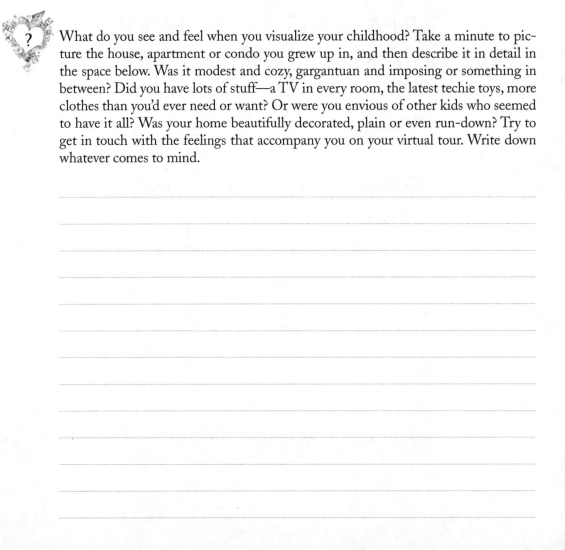

What do you see and feel when you visualize your childhood? Take a minute to picture the house, apartment or condo you grew up in, and then describe it in detail in the space below. Was it modest and cozy, gargantuan and imposing or something in between? Did you have lots of stuff—a TV in every room, the latest techie toys, more clothes than you'd ever need or want? Or were you envious of other kids who seemed to have it all? Was your home beautifully decorated, plain or even run-down? Try to get in touch with the feelings that accompany you on your virtual tour. Write down whatever comes to mind.

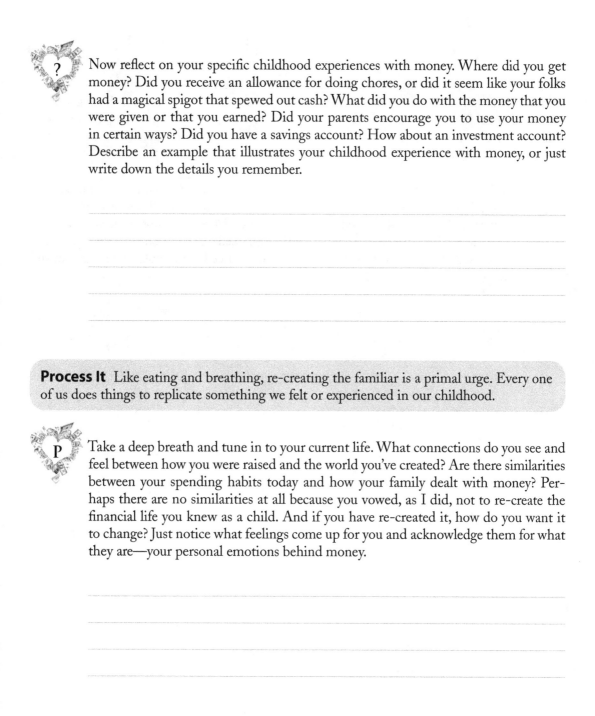

Now reflect on your specific childhood experiences with money. Where did you get money? Did you receive an allowance for doing chores, or did it seem like your folks had a magical spigot that spewed out cash? What did you do with the money that you were given or that you earned? Did your parents encourage you to use your money in certain ways? Did you have a savings account? How about an investment account? Describe an example that illustrates your childhood experience with money, or just write down the details you remember.

**Process It** Like eating and breathing, re-creating the familiar is a primal urge. Every one of us does things to replicate something we felt or experienced in our childhood.

Take a deep breath and tune in to your current life. What connections do you see and feel between how you were raised and the world you've created? Are there similarities between your spending habits today and how your family dealt with money? Perhaps there are no similarities at all because you vowed, as I did, not to re-create the financial life you knew as a child. And if you have re-created it, how do you want it to change? Just notice what feelings come up for you and acknowledge them for what they are—your personal emotions behind money.

# STAYING IN TOUCH WITH YOURSELF

I've come to believe that most unhealthy behaviors are the result of two types of emotional conflict within an individual: first, having needs that aren't met and second, having trouble setting personal boundaries, which allows a person's sense of self to be violated. This exercise will help deepen your awareness of how these conflicts are working beneath the surface of your life.

When was the last time you created space in your day to be alone with your thoughts? Sit quietly for a few minutes now and listen to your own heartbeat. Just breathe and ask yourself, "What do I need? What do I want?" Maybe it's more time alone or with certain family members or friends. Maybe you need a creative outlet or more physical activity. Allow yourself to acknowledge whatever needs and wants come to mind, and write them below.

Now think about specific, practical ways you might meet one of the needs or desires you listed. Do you need fifteen minutes of alone time each day when you get home from work before you can calmly join the rest of your family? Do you need a friend or your spouse to listen to you vent about something without commenting, judging or problem-solving? Do you need to begin an exercise program? Choose one of the needs that you've listed above and describe how you might meet it in the near future.

**Reflect On It** Modern life doesn't allow us the luxury of time to sort out our feelings or to calm our minds enough to think about our wants and needs. We go from one event to another with little decompression time, only to explode or implode later when those wants or needs aren't fulfilled. We've all ignored or numbed our feelings for the sake of taking care of the "necessities." But just as our bodies respond positively to bicycling or jogging, our minds respond positively to stimulus, exercise and release—and the solitude or peace to find these things.

# STAYING IN TOUCH WITH YOURSELF
## PART II

As children, we're taught that setting personal boundaries is selfish. Still, you know in your heart of hearts if something is or is not acceptable to you; you're either comfortable with it or you're not.

Give yourself a few minutes right now to think of a time in the recent past when you went along with something even though you felt it wasn't acceptable.

_____

_____

_____

_____

Try to appreciate that you had good reasons for acting the way you did. Now try to pinpoint why you chose to let the situation slide. What did you think might happen if you stood up for what you thought was right? Answer in the most self-accepting and forgiving way you can.

_____

_____

_____

_____

_____

In what ways did the experience violate your sense of self? Did you later feel you had been dishonest? Did you feel hurt but refuse to show it? Describe how your actions conflicted with your values.

_____

_____

_____

_____

_____

What are some different ways you might deal with a similar situation in the future? Think of solutions that fit your personality and communication style. If you're normally a reserved person, sudden confrontation in a public place probably doesn't fit your style. Describe the details of what you might say and do in a way that feels real and right to you.

_____

_____

_____

_____

# YOUR FINANCIAL BLIND SPOT

## *EBM* Exercise 9

Read through the composites of the Financial Personalities below. Check the boxes next to any qualities that ring true to you. Answer as honestly as you can.

Hoarders

- ☐ are territorial when it comes to sharing things with others.
- ☐ were typically givers when they were younger.
- ☐ stockpile stuff (and emotions) for fear that they will be snatched by others.
- ☐ may have come from scarcity when they were younger.

Spenders

- ☐ spend their money as quickly as it comes in.
- ☐ have amassed substantial credit card debt.
- ☐ have clothes and gadgets they seldom use.
- ☐ feel temporary emotional relief when spending money.

Saboteurs

- ☐ constantly fluctuate between hoarding and spending.
- ☐ consciously believe they can be successful.
- ☐ unconsciously believe they don't deserve financial abundance.
- ☐ surround themselves with people who lack ambition and drive.

Givers

- ☐ are wonderfully warm and generous.
- ☐ have a hard time receiving.
- ☐ are likely to be attracted to spenders and hoarders.
- ☐ are forever trying to fill someone else's bucket.

Controllers

- ☐ are frugal in nature.
- ☐ manage their financial affairs themselves, to the smallest detail.
- ☐ are typically not mindful of their personal relationships.
- ☐ are micromanagers and often miss the big picture.

Planners

- ☐ find comfort in plotting how to get from point A to point B.
- ☐ are not spontaneous with money.
- ☐ live in the future rather than in the present moment.
- ☐ are knocked off balance when the unexpected happens.

Carefree Butterflies

- ☐ think things will always somehow work out.
- ☐ are healthy and happy in all aspects of life.
- ☐ live in the present moment.
- ☐ are often disconnected from their money.

Attractors

- ☐ are successful without really trying.
- ☐ profit from every venture they set their minds to.
- ☐ are open to the flow of giving and receiving in life.
- ☐ have a healthy relationship with money.

# YOUR FINACIAL BLIND SPOT
*(continued)*

**Process It** After completing the checklist, sit quietly for a few moments, just focusing on breathing in and out. Then answer the questions below without judging yourself or anyone else. Just think about and listen to what your heart is saying.

**P** Which of the details you marked in the checklist hit closest to home? What were you most surprised to recognize in your own financial behavior?

_____

_____

_____

_____

**P** Reflect back on the last month or pay period. What was going on inside you emotionally? How did those feelings, happy, sad or otherwise, affect your financial behavior? Did they get transferred onto your Visa card? Did your feelings affect the company you kept? Did your financial personality change based on the company you kept? Describe the connection between your emotions and your financial behavior in as much detail as you can.

_____

_____

_____

_____

_____

_____

_____

_____

**P** Search your mind for parallels between your current financial patterns and your up-bringing. Describe how those relationships or tribal rules and beliefs still influence your financial independence.

_____

_____

_____

_____

_____

_____

_____

_____

**P** What do you think would happen if you were to break away from certain financial habits? How do you think you would feel if you changed? How do you think your family and friends would react if you changed?

_____

_____

_____

_____

_____

_____

_____

_____

# SURVIVING TO THRIVING

## *EBM* Exercise 10

According to the gifted psychologist Mary Ann Daly, as we recover from personal tragedy, grief, loss, abuse and trauma, we move from feeling like Victims to Survivors to Thrivers. Just as people with histories of childhood trauma need to move through the stages of recovery to create a new emotional infrastructure, so do people with toxic emotional relationships with money.

In the **Victim** stage we tend to feel stuck, helpless, hopeless, depressed, overwhelmed, afraid and angry.

In the **Survivor** stage we tend to feel more hopeful, motivated and aware, though still unstable.

In the **Thriver** stage we tend to feel focused, grateful, joyful and accepting of change.

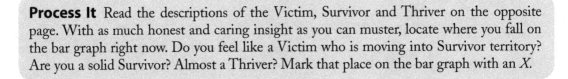

**Process It** Read the descriptions of the Victim, Survivor and Thriver on the opposite page. With as much honest and caring insight as you can muster, locate where you fall on the bar graph right now. Do you feel like a Victim who is moving into Survivor territory? Are you a solid Survivor? Almost a Thriver? Mark that place on the bar graph with an *X*.

**I feel like a Victim.**

I think and speak negatively.

I see things in black and white.

I am usually either depressed or anxious.

I am chronically sick or feel disconnected from my body.

I don't see the options to get out of difficult situations.

I protect myself through denial, justification, aggression, repression, acting out or fantasizing.

I trust people who aren't worthy of my trust.

I don't trust myself.

I have little or no sense of my purpose in life.

**I feel like a Survivor.**

I still feel competitive with other people.

I still have difficulty respecting or creating healthy boundaries.

I am less anxious and depressed lately.

I've been taking better care of myself physically.

I notice I keep repeating the same destructive patterns.

I feel hopeful and ready to change.

I am beginning to trust myself.

I have a new sense of purpose in my life.

**I feel like a Thriver.**

I am consistently able to express myself in healthy ways.

I have clear and solid boundaries.

I recognize and honor my own and other people's limitations.

I welcome change as an opportunity to grow.

I display gratitude and appreciation regularly.

I have a clear sense of purpose.

I have faith that somehow I will be taken care of.

I feel a strong connection to my spirit and to the universe.

# SURVIVING TO THRIVING

*(continued)*

Review the profiles of the eight Financial Personalities from earlier in the chapter. Choose a characteristic you recognize as especially strong in you and list it under "Current Financial Behaviors" in the space below. Then list a few examples of situations in which you exhibited that characteristic. For example, I recognize myself as a Giver. The sentence that says "Givers have a hard time receiving" really strikes a chord with me. I can think of countless times in my life when I felt uncomfortable receiving from others, from birthday gifts to professional accolades. Write down as many scenarios as you can think of. Be specific. Incorporate names and locations if you need to.

Current Financial Behaviors

When you've explored several of your Financial Personality traits, I'd like you to turn your attention to the space below, labeled "New Behaviors." Here, write down a different response that you could have exhibited in each situation you listed under "Current Financial Behaviors." For example, when I received my first sales award, instead of downplaying my colleagues' congratulatory remarks, I could have smiled and thanked them graciously. Or I could have told my boss that I'm uncomfortable with public recognition and I'd rather he not make a big to-do about it. The point is that I have choices, and so do you. Even if you're the biggest Spender or Planner or Controller you know, you have choices in your day-to-day financial behavior. So go ahead—see if there are some habits you'd like to change.

New Behaviors

# BREAKING AWAY FROM INHERITED BELIEFS: TYING IT ALL TOGETHER

We each have an emotional infrastructure that may need repair in order for us to process the feelings that arise from unmet needs and weak boundaries. This emotional infrastructure, especially where money is concerned, can be damaged by our upbringing. Our upbringing and our ability to deal with conflict are the factors that create our Financial Personality. By focusing on changing our financial behavior, even in small ways, we begin to change our Financial Personality and progress from a life of victimhood or survival mode to a life of thriving and abundance.

My Financial Personality is _____,

but I would like to work on _____.

| My unmet needs and desires include the following: | I would like to have stronger boundaries in the following areas: | I can change my financial behavior in these specific, small ways: |
| --- | --- | --- |
| | | |

# SECTION TWO
## Choose to Change

# OWN YOUR PERSONAL POWER

*"Every human has four endowments—
self awareness, conscience, independent will
and creative imagination. These give us the
ultimate human freedom...the power to
choose, to respond, to change."*

—Stephen Covey

# CHOOSE TO CHANGE
### *The Emotion Behind Money* **Exercise 11**

Your future is your choice; you're the designer. What's it going to be? What positive financial choices would you like to make? What unhealthy financial choices and behaviors would you like to change or completely let go? Be loving toward yourself as you consider what you dislike about your current reality. Think of your dislikes as familiar items you've outgrown, like childhood toys, old furniture or clothing. Feel yourself letting them go. Close your eyes for a minute and let your mind explore the possibilities. Then set your intentions by writing each behavior as a completion of this statement: *I choose to* —————.


Here are some suggestions:

"I choose to love myself enough to make healthy financial choices."

"I choose to live within my means."

"I choose to face my current financial reality."


Or you can simply state your intent:

"I choose to save $100 a month for six months."

"I choose to have a positive relationship with money."

"I choose to have wealth in abundance."

Write your own intentions in the spaces provided below. Continue on the blank lines if you need to. Try to frame your choices in a positive light, in terms of what you want rather than what you don't want. (For example, "I choose to save $100 per month" rather than "I choose to stop spending money on clothes I don't need.")

I choose to _____ .

I choose to _____ .

I choose to _____ .

I choose to _____ .

I choose to _____ .

_____

_____

**Process It** The possibilities are endless because they're your possibilities! You just have to invite the possibilities to become realities.

 After you've made your list, look it over. Pick as many choice statements as you like and write them down on sticky notes. These are your reminders of how you choose to live, financially or otherwise. Post them in places where you'll see them every day. Have fun with it. Heck, plaster your home and office with colorful notes if you like.

 Repeat these intentions to yourself throughout the day. Before you know it, those conscious choices will be transformed into new behaviors and a new reality.

# POSITIVE PERSPECTIVE

Life is all in how you look at it. The way you perceive yourself is the way you'll present yourself to the world. If you see yourself as the victim, the martyr, the hero, the child, the rich man, the poor woman, that's who you'll become.

 What are the roles you feel you're destined to play in life? Are you the caretaker, the comedian, the entrepreneur, the leader, the teacher, the mentor? List your roles in the left column of the chart below. List whatever pros and cons you can recognize for each role. Be as honest and thorough as you can. Pros for a caretaking role might include appreciation from others and a feeling of doing good. Cons might include that the role is time-consuming and often thankless.

| ROLE | PROS | CONS |
| --- | --- | --- |
|  |  |  |

**Process It**  A few years ago, I made a conscious choice to keep a positive perspective on things. Being happy was not my nature when I started out. It was something I had to teach myself, a choice I made and still make every day. What choices can you make to change your perspective?

P  Look at the answers you wrote in the chart on the previous page. List the roles that have few pros and many cons.

_____

_____

_____

_____

P  What would happen if you dropped these roles from your repertoire? Empowering, isn't it?

_____

_____

_____

_____

_____

_____

_____

# TWO SIDES TO EVERYTHING

The image below is one of those pictures that plays tricks with your mind. Depending on how you look at it, you see either the profile of a beautiful young woman or an old woman with a big nose. I find it amazing that the same image can literally depict two different realities.

**Reflect On It** Your life is in this drawing. The image that you focus on first is your current reality. When you choose to shift your perspective, you see things differently. Similarly, a shift in your perception about money yields a different outcome.

Having a truly positive perspective means being able to understand where other people are com-ing from. As Steven Covey says in his book *The Seven Habits of Highly Effective People* (1989), the world would be an amazing place if more people would first seek to understand and then to be understood. Take a crack at shifting your perspective in this way.

Describe your side of a conflict or an argument you had with someone recently. What were your interests and goals? How was the other person standing in your way?

Now try to imagine what the other person's perspective might have been. Describe his or her side of the argument as fairly and evenhandedly as you can. Try to see that person's perspective as different from yours, motivated by different goals, rather than right or wrong.

How did it feel to try to imagine the other perspective? Did the shift come naturally to you? Was it difficult? Did the attempt make you feel nervous, calm, confused, liberated? What do you understand differently about the argument now?

# TAKE YOUR PASSION
# AND MAKE IT HAPPEN
### *EBM* Exercise 12

Imagine what your life would be like if you never felt anything was untouchable or out of reach. What if the power of your intentions, thoughts and words could actually become your reality? What if, when you choose to live a certain life, think of yourself living that life and talk as if it already existed, it becomes real?

 What would you like to do but feel you'll never have the money to do? Don't be shy. Live it up! Give yourself permission to make a big list in the left column of the chart on the opposite page.

 In the middle column of the chart, next to each item you listed in the left column, write down the specific reason you don't think you have the money for it. For example, let's say you answered that you've always wanted to rent a villa for a month in Tuscany. Perhaps the reason you don't have the money reads something like this: "I have one kid in college and one in private school. I don't make that kind of money."

 Revisit each reason in the middle column of the chart, and in the right column, re-write your response with a positive thought. For example, change "I don't make that kind of money" to "I should look into payment options for next semester" or "Can my family donate time at school events to offset tuition costs?" Be creative!

| I WOULD LIKE TO | I CAN'T BECAUSE | POSITIVE RESPONSE |
|---|---|---|
| | | |

# GRATEFUL MOMENTS

My boss and mentor Bob Lyman saw that I was letting life get the best of me and that it was affecting my work. As an antidote, he said I would have to tell him every day, even on weekends, five things I was grateful for, or else I'd be fired. In hindsight, I realize it was a simple and effective way to keep me focused on the positive. And it worked! Teaching me to be grateful every day and to put those thoughts into words really did shift my consciousness to a more positive outlook. It was one of the greatest gifts I've ever received.

 What five things are you grateful for today?

1.

2.

3.

4.

5.

**Process It** Consider taking a few minutes each day, either all at once or sprinkled throughout the day, to express your gratitude. Here are some small ways to recognize the positive and give it power.

 Keep a "Gratitude Journal" as a place to record the gifts that life gives you on a daily basis.

Say "thank you" for the little things that people do for you.

In the midst of a bad situation, try to find something to be grateful for.

Make arrangements with a Gratitude Buddy—your spouse, one of your kids or a co-worker—to exchange short lists of what you're grateful for each day for a month.

# SETTING YOURSELFT UP FOR SUCCESS

You can actually set yourself up to be lucky—or at least to avoid many of the bad-luck scenarios that in the financial arena can trap you in a cycle of struggling for survival. Position yourself to be lucky. If you own a home, create a Home Fund, where you save for inevitable repairs like purchasing a new roof or a hot-water heater. I've always wanted a boat, so I started a Boat Fund. I put aside a set amount every month. In fact, I have many funds set up in electronic savings accounts so that when a bill comes due, I already have the money. It's fun to watch a fund grow!

**?** What are the areas in your financial life where you know you'll benefit from putting a little away each month or even each paycheck?

_____

_____

_____

Life is full of surprises. Position yourself to be lucky by making payments to yourself out of your cash flow for things you've already paid off. Once you're done with your $400 per month car payment, for example, save that money to fund your next car. I call this the Autopilot Plan. It's empowering to be your own bank!

**?** What areas of your financial life could you put on the Autopilot Plan?

_____

_____

_____

**Reflect On It**  Only 5 percent of Americans save first and then spend. These are the people who hold the most wealth in this country. Which side of the fence do you want to be on?

# OWN YOUR PERSONAL POWER:
# TYING IT ALL TOGETHER

It comes down to this: you have the power to alter the course of your life by choosing to think, speak and act in positive, proactive ways rather than negative, reactive ways. That means reframing negative thoughts, appreciating the richness of life and recognizing realities other than the one that first appears to you.

Use the three small boxes in the chart below to record three specific ways in which your perspective has shifted from negative to positive. In the large box, draw some conclusions about how these shifts in perspective have opened a world of promise and unlimited possibilities to you.

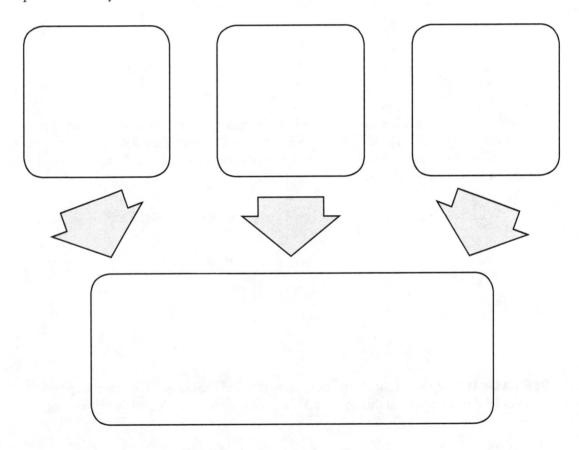

# YOUR TURNING POINT

*"You must be the change you
wish to see in the world."*

—Mohandas Gandhi

# YOUR DREAM LIST

A couple of years ago, my husband, Billy, began obsessing over his perception that he'd done nothing in his life. He just couldn't get past his feelings of inadequacy and shame. I decided it was time for him to make a list of what he had dreamed of doing since he was a kid. I grabbed a piece of scrap paper and said, "Okay, time to make your dream list." Soon he had a list of all kinds of great things, including attending a Notre Dame football game, going to a Big Ten football game, using his vacation days to actually leave town, going to Europe and much more.

Billy had never before considered that he could reach out and grab each and every one of these dreams. But he did. Over the following year he went down his list and knocked off each desire, one at a time. As he did, he was able to shrug off the weight of those unfulfilled dreams and do things that moved his soul. When his first list was completed, he began to tackle other life dreams.

**Process It** Many of us go through life without pursuing our passions—big or small. We have the perception that these things are unobtainable, but it is just that: a *perception*. Give yourself permission to start small. As you find yourself achieving the little things on your dream list, bigger dreams will start to seem more within your reach. And living your dreams yields a life of no regrets—unquestionably one of the greatest characteristics of an abundant and rewarding life.

Now I invite you to make a list like Billy did. Stop and ponder the things you've always wanted to do. Feel the excitement welling up inside as you write them down. They're all there for the taking. Come on, grab them! When you're done, give yourself a timeline to actually accomplish everything on your list—six months, a year, five years. It doesn't matter. It's your list, and it's time to bring it on!

## MY DREAM LIST                    IDEAL GOAL DATE

# LIFE TRANFORMATION
### *The Emotion Behind Money* Exercise 13

I've found that in order to create a life of abundance, you must first define your ideal life. To do so, you must tune in to your Inner Wealth. In chapter 1, we talked about the Life Navigation Wheel, and I pointed out that when we put work or money at the center of the wheel, we're perpetually scraping and saving to maintain a certain lifestyle or achieve a better "someday."

Now I'd like you to start thinking of your wheel as having your life's purpose, or Inner Wealth, at the center, with the other four circles orbiting it. When you do this, you shift your focus away from money. Instead, you're motivated by what you want out of life. This is the foundation for a life of thriving. You're now ready to tune in to your Inner Wealth and create a wheel of your own.

The first thing I'd like you to do is sit quietly. Breathe deeply and listen to the beat of your heart. Follow its rhythm. Feel its strength. Picture yourself sitting with your eyes closed, face tilted upward to the sun. Drink in the warmth and heat. Absorb it into every pore. Follow the warmth through your limbs, into your core. Feel the energy and power of your true self. Think about the values and principles you stand for. Consider the things that are important to you. Ponder your special gifts and abilities. Take a few more deep breaths and open your eyes.

Use the diagram of the Life Navigation Wheel on the next page to help you complete the four parts of the exercise that follow.

I know the concept of reaching for your dreams can be difficult to comprehend, but join me. Join me in the stratosphere for a moment and consider lofty notions such as the values you hold dear—for example, happiness, peace, pure bliss. Dream of what you'd like to see happen in your life, no matter how wacky it may seem. Think about it from every possible angle. Be sure to be authentic in your responses.

# LIFE NAVIGATION WHEEL

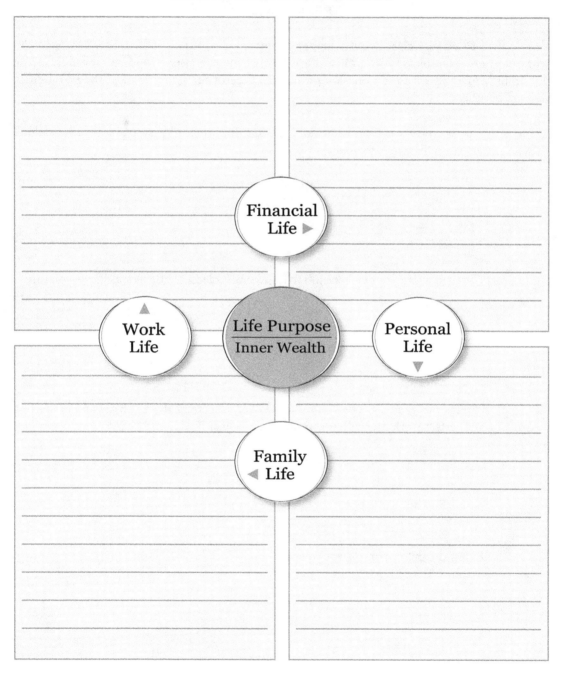

# PART ONE: YOUR WORK LIFE
## *EBM* Exercise 14

People tend to be very clear about whether or not they love their jobs. If you love your job without reservation, please move on to Part Two of the exercise. If not, answer each of the questions below. Sit with each one for a moment. Open your mind to all of the possibilities that are out there.

What do you *really* want to be doing as your livelihood? What type of work wouldn't even seem like work to you?

_____

_____

What is it about your current job that gives you pleasure? Be as specific as you can.

_____

_____

Think about the past jobs you've had. What aspects of those jobs would be part of your perfect work life? What about those jobs just made time fly by?

_____

_____

Do you dream of working for yourself?　　☐ Yes　☐ No
Explain why you answered the way you did.

_____

_____

What do others say you're really great at? Why do you think they say that? If you're not sure, ask them!

_____

_____

_____

_____

 What do others say you should have been? Why do you think they say that?

_____

_____

_____

_____

**Process It**  Now I'd like you to picture yourself doing something you truly love. Go ahead and create a scene in your head. Imagine that you're getting paid for it. Actually picture yourself at the bank depositing the income from your business or looking at that paycheck from the job you love. Feel the satisfaction and gratitude in your heart that comes from knowing you're financially rewarded for doing what you do best.

 When you're ready, refer back to the diagram of the Life Navigation Wheel on page 75. Next to the circle labeled "Work Life," I'd like you to write down how you see your ideal work life. How does it look? How does it feel?" Be as descriptive and detailed as you can.

# PART TWO: YOUR FAMILY LIFE

What is a family, anyway? These days, having a family is not necessarily defined as having blood relatives. Your family might be made up of people you love, with whom you share a spiritual bond. Which of the following statements describe your family life? Check as many as apply.

## FOR SINGLES

☐ My friends are my family.

☐ My extended family (parents, grand-parents, aunts, uncles, cousins) is very important to me.

☐ I want very much to have a partner or spouse.

☐ I'm ready to get married and start a family.

☐ I want to have a child.

☐ I want to help others and remain single.

☐ I spend quite a bit of time envying other people's family ties.

☐ _____

☐ _____

☐ _____

## FOR PARTNERED

☐ I dream of escaping a relationship that's not feeding my soul.

☐ My extended family (parents, grand-parents, aunts, uncles, cousins) is very important to me.

☐ I long to spend more time with my kids or my nieces and nephews.

☐ I would prefer to be a family with one income versus two in order to have one spouse raise our children.

☐ I would prefer to remain childless.

☐ I spend quite a bit of time envying other people's family ties.

☐ _____

☐ _____

☐ _____

Are you beginning to imagine your ideal family life? Great! Now consider the questions below and answer them as carefully and honestly as you can.

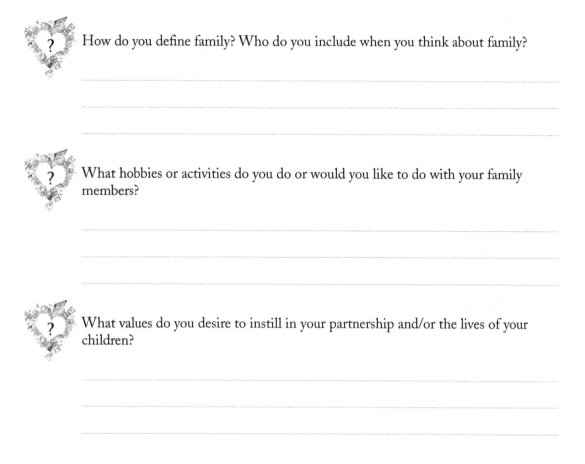

How do you define family? Who do you include when you think about family?

_____

_____

What hobbies or activities do you do or would you like to do with your family members?

_____

_____

_____

What values do you desire to instill in your partnership and/or the lives of your children?

_____

_____

_____

**Process It** Whatever your story, the key is to dream about your family life the way *you* want it to be. It's the only life you have, and you deserve to make the best of it.

When you're ready, turn back to the Life Navigation Wheel on page 75. Next to the Family Life circle, record your ideal family life. Describe it exactly as you want it to look and feel, down to the last detail.

# PART THREE: YOUR PERSONAL LIFE

How much time do you spend doing things that feed your soul, activities that benefit you and only you? It's time to focus on your health, your hobbies and your overall well-being. Read through the list below and check any items that feel true to you.

☐ I wish I could do more for my overall health.

☐ I'd like to feel more awake and energetic on a daily basis.

☐ I'd love to be in better physical shape.

☐ Losing some weight would be a good idea.

☐ I could only benefit from loving and appreciating myself more.

☐ I've always wanted to learn to meditate or do yoga.

☐ I wish I had more time to spend with friends.

☐ Travel is one of the most important things in the world to me.

☐ I wish I knew how to cook and eat more healthfully.

☐ I dream of running a marathon.

☐ I'd prefer to have more time alone.

☐ I would be so excited to act or sing in local theatrical productions.

☐ I long to disappear for a while to write a book.

☐ Learning to play an instrument would make me so happy.

☐ I wish I could go back to school.

☐ Other: _____

_____

_____

Now that you have some general ideas about how you might spend your time outside of family, work and money commitments, it's time to begin thinking about the specific details of your ideal personal life. Answer the questions here as authentically as you possibly can. This is your ideal life we're talking about, so don't hold back!

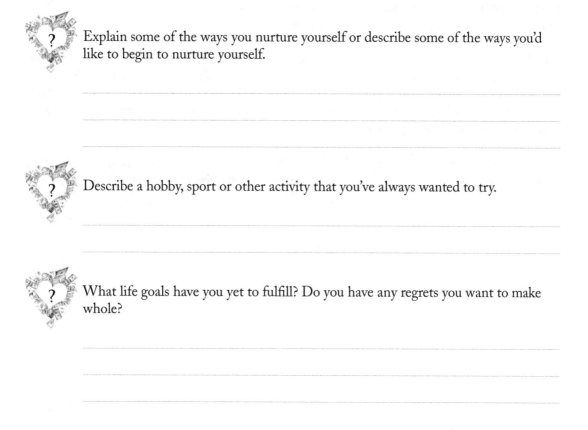

? Explain some of the ways you nurture yourself or describe some of the ways you'd like to begin to nurture yourself.

_____

_____

_____

? Describe a hobby, sport or other activity that you've always wanted to try.

_____

_____

? What life goals have you yet to fulfill? Do you have any regrets you want to make whole?

_____

_____

_____

**Process It** What would you like to make a priority in your personal life? Maybe you want to do things that aren't necessarily about achievement or completing a task. Maybe you want to shift from *doing* to *being* by creating a more balanced or harmonic life.

P Take a few moments to crystallize what your ideal personal life would look like. When you're ready, return to the Life Navigation Wheel on page 75 and write down the details next to the Personal Life circle. Include goals, challenges, achievements—whatever excites you.

# PART FOUR: YOUR FINANCIAL LIFE

Are you seeking financial independence?
Do you want to get a handle on your cash flow?
Do you want to reduce your financial commitments to others?
Do you dream of being massively generous to those less fortunate than you?

As odd as it may seem, your financial life is one of the areas I like to call "the warm and fuzzies," because I believe it is directly linked to your heart. Your financial life—what you do with the money you accumulate—is where you begin designing your future. Be honest with yourself as you think about your financial ideal and answer the questions below. And remember, only positive self-talk allowed!

What financial life do you dream of? Do you dream of providing a college education for your children? Do you want to create your own foundation? It's all up to you!

_____

_____

_____

_____

_____

_____

_____

What type of accumulation goals do you have, and what specifically are you doing to fulfill them?

_____

_____

_____

_____

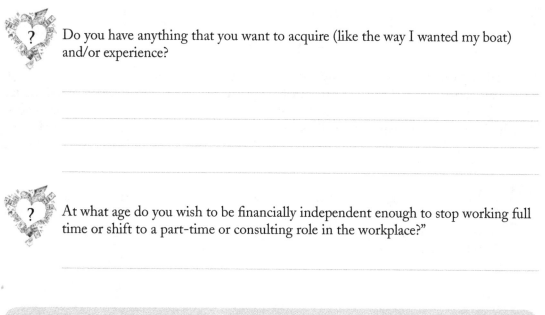

? Do you have anything that you want to acquire (like the way I wanted my boat) and/or experience?

_____

_____

_____

_____

? At what age do you wish to be financially independent enough to stop working full time or shift to a part-time or consulting role in the workplace?"

_____

**Process It** What does your ideal financial life look like? I encourage you to think outside the box here. What does it look like? What does it feel like? Remember: It can be yours if you can visualize it and feel it as if you've already reached your goal. Don't hold back!

P When you feel ready, go back to the Life Navigation Wheel on page 75 and describe your ideal Financial Life beside the circle. Imagine it down to the last detail.

# LIFE STAGES VISUALIZATION
## *EBM* Exercise 15

Our modern lives move through many stages (education, dating, career, marriage, parenthood, retirement, to name a few). At each juncture between stages, our life's purpose changes, and it's crucial that we consciously redefine it. Visualize your life from the perspective of life stages. Which experiences and emotions defined each stage? How have you moved through each stage to get to where you are today? Answer the following questions with as much insight and self-acceptance as you can muster.

**?** Visualize the trajectory of your life so far. Take a few moments to sink into the emotions you felt at each stage. Describe the highlights of what you feel have been the most important stages. If you want to get creative, give each stage a fun title, such as "The Dating Years."

_____

_____

_____

_____

_____

_____

_____

_____

**?** Are you at a transition point in your life now (for example, about to be married, about to have your first child, about to retire)? If so, describe the transition.

_____

_____

_____

What do you want the next phase of your life to look and feel like? Use the space below in whatever way helps you visualize it. What you visualize is exactly what you'll manifest! If it helps, cut out pictures that illustrate your ideal life. Or if you're talented like my sisters Marianne and Katie, draw your ideal world. Have fun with it, go crazy, be creative— but by all means be positive.

**Reflect On It** Remember: thoughts and emotions become facts. The energy you put out attracts similar energy. Sense that energetic pull. No matter what, don't waste another minute of your life wondering if you'll have enough money to live your dreams. State your intentions for your money clearly and positively.

# YOUR TURNING POINT:
# TYING IT ALL TOGETHER

The world around us teaches that power is achieved through financial gain. I believe the opposite is true—that if you retain your personal power and live your life focused on your true self, your life will be overflowing with money.

I'm here to help you make financial decisions based on who *you* are and where *you* want to go. But this is a two-way street. Documenting your dreams is the first step toward achieving those personal goals. You cannot progress from surviving to thriving without acknowledging your ideal life and creating a plan to realize those ideals.

**Process It**   Review your completed Life Navigation Wheel on page 75. Then sit quietly for a minute and imagine how the descriptions you wrote there might manifest themselves in your everyday life. What would a scene from your ideal life look like, sound like, feel like?

 Use the dream cloud on the following page to write or draw a description of an ideal moment, scene or day in your life, based on the descriptions you wrote on your Life Navigation Wheel.

**Reflect On It** If you've completed the exercises in this workbook thus far, you've just arrived at an important milestone in your journey toward abundance: your financial turning point. You're now separated from the pack. You're poised to build *your* wealth in order to achieve the life that *you* want for yourself and your family, today and in the future. If you're living your life's purpose and apportioning your money according to your desired intentions, you have set yourself up to be lucky, and abundance can be yours.

6

# THE CRABS IN YOUR BUCKET

*"Attitude is a little thing
that makes a big difference."*

—Winston Churchill

# RECOGNIZING YOUR CRABS

If you've ever visited the shore and seen how live crabs behave, you know exactly where the metaphor "crabs in a bucket" comes from. If you put one crab in a bucket, it can climb out by itself, no problem. But if you fill the bucket with twenty crabs, just as one gets to the rim, the other crabs pull it back down.

You'll get no trouble from the other crabs as long as you stay in the bucket with them. However, as you begin to climb out by listening to your Inner Wealth and taking steps to follow your heart's desires, you're likely to feel the crabs in your bucket try to pull you back down. Some of the crabs in your bucket might be the people you know and love, and some might be living in-side your head, in the form of your own fears and insecurities. Other crabs, like time and money constraints, might be abstract or material influences.

**Reflect On It** I used to let the crabs in my bucket get the best of me. When I returned to the south side of Chicago after college graduation, people I'd grown up with and been around all of my life called me a traitor and a north-side snob for driving a new Honda, for living downtown and even for being slim and healthy. Their reaction fed my insecurities to the point that I gained back all the weight I'd lost, and then some! Because I didn't recognize them as the crabs in my bucket, doing what comes naturally, I allowed my loved ones too much control over my personal power. I realize now that the issue was me. At that time I wasn't able to hold boundaries with others, and I allowed their attitudes to affect me.

 Consider the crabs in your bucket. Think about the times you've felt resistance from friends or loved ones in the past, especially when making decisions that were truly healthy for you. Have you changed plans to suit other people even at your own expense? Have you avoided doing what is best for you because you were afraid or because you lacked confidence in yourself? Think about which of your own fears and insecurities have pulled you back down into your bucket.

# *WHAT* IS KEEPING YOU OFF TRACK?

Some of the obstacles that can appear as crabs in your bucket are time, money, debt levels and interest rates. Read through the statements in each category below. Which of them feel true to you? Check the box next to any statement that applies to your life.

## TIME

☐ I often complain about a lack of time.

☐ I feel as though I hardly have a minute to eat or rest.

☐ I would like to feel more productive.

☐ I'm frequently distracted from the task at hand.

☐ I have difficulty saying no when people ask me to do something.

☐ I'm always behind in my work or in reaching my personal goals.

☐ Other: _____

### CLAIM IT!

☐ Time is one of the crabs in my bucket. My perspective on time is an obstacle on the road to my dreams and desires.

**Process It** As a person with an often hectic schedule, I've found tremendous value in making time for meditation. The more time I devote to it, the calmer and more productive I am. Meditation can take many different forms. For you, meditation might mean running on a treadmill, taking a walk around the neighborhood, watching the sun set, praying or using a mantra—think of it as whatever helps you to calm your mind and connect with your soul.

Take a few minutes right now and list some of the ways you might meditate. What makes you feel peaceful, relaxed and centered?

_____

_____

_____

# *WHAT* IS KEEPING YOU OFF TRACK?

*(continued)*

## MONEY/CASH FLOW

☐ There was a time when I earned very little income.

☐ I make more money than ever, but I still feel strapped.

☐ I can't afford to live the way I'd like to.

☐ My lifestyle has grown more elaborate as I've earned more money.

☐ I have little or no money saved.

☐ When I retire, I want to travel and have fun.

☐ Other: _____

### CLAIM IT!

☐ Money is one of the crabs in my bucket. I feel stuck on the treadmill of earning to maintain my lifestyle.


## DEBT LEVEL AND INTEREST RATES

☐ In the past I've considered debt just part of the modern lifestyle.

☐ I've taken on debt pretty casually in the past.

☐ It seems hard or impossible to get ahead financially.

☐ If I lost my job or became seriously ill tomorrow, I'd be unable to pay my debts.

☐ I don't think much about the cumulative interest I'm paying on my debts.

☐ Some or all of the interest rates on my debts are variable rather than fixed.

☐ Other: _____

### CLAIM IT!

☐ Debt is one of the crabs in my bucket. I've taken on debt without really considering the implications.

# FINANCIAL JARGON

Do you shy away from conversations with your financial advisor because it's so difficult to understand what he or she is really saying? If so, your financial advisor might be speaking in fi-nancial jargon, the gibberish financial folks use when talking about their products and services, numbers, rates, percentages and the like. Do you avoid learning more about your investments because the subject just seems too complicated? Is it possible that you might be missing out on investment opportunities because you don't really know or understand your options? Are you in touch with your risk tolerance? Have you considered all the variables when planning for re-tirement? Financial jargon and misperceptions might be crabs in your bucket. Check the boxes below that apply to your situation.

☐ I don't really understand how my investments work.

☐ I don't understand my investment, savings and insurance options very well.

☐ My employer had a financial professional come in to educate staff about our investments, but it didn't help me much.

☐ My eyes glaze over when my financial advisor talks about my portfolio.

☐ I might not understand my financial advisors, but I trust that they know what they're doing.

☐ Other: _____

## CLAIM IT!

☐ Financial jargon is one of the crabs in my bucket. I feel confused about investing my money.

# *WHAT* IS KEEPING YOU OFF TRACK?

*(continued)*

## MISPERCEPTIONS

☐ I've been under the impression that I need a lot of money to have a professionally managed investment account.

☐ I'm not sure if my financial advisor has access to a full array of investment options.

☐ I don't feel as if my investments match my risk tolerance.

☐ I have few or no investments outside the stock and bond markets.

☐ I thought real estate wasn't a viable investment for everyday people.

☐ Other: _____

### CLAIM IT!

☐ Misperception about investment options is one of the crabs in my bucket. I've had certain ideas about investing my money that might not be true.

## FEAR OF RISK OR ADDICTION TO RISK

☐ My financial advisor follows an investment formula for people my age.

☐ I'm not sure what kind of risk I'm emotionally comfortable with when it comes to my investments.

☐ When my investments lose money, I have an uncomfortable emotional reaction.

☐ I would feel comfortable having more aggressive growth investments in my portfolio.

☐ Other: _____

### CLAIM IT!

☐ Fear of risk or addiction to risk is one of the crabs in my bucket. My risk tolerance doesn't seem to match my portfolio.

# LACK OF RETIREMENT INCOME PLANNING

☐ I'm quite nervous about the financial realities of retirement.

☐ I'm not sure that I'm set for retirement financially.

☐ I plan to maintain the same lifestyle I have now during retirement.

☐ I haven't really considered inflation and longevity when planning my retirement.

☐ Other: _____

## CLAIM IT!

☐ Lack of retirement income planning is one of the crabs in my bucket. There are some financial aspects of retirement that I haven't considered yet.

# *WHO* IS KEEPING YOU OFF TRACK?

By now I'm sure you understand it isn't just what is holding you back, it's who. Who are the crabs pulling you back down into the bucket as you try to express your Inner Wealth? Do the members of your family, your friends, your co-workers and your employer want you to live the life they envision for you rather than the one you envision for yourself? Be as honest as you can as you read the statements below and check those that are true for you.

## FAMILY, FRIENDS, CO-WORKERS, EMPLOYER

☐ It is very important to me to please my parents or other close family members.

☐ One or more of my friends has seemed upset when I make decisions I know will be beneficial to me in a healthy way.

☐ My co-workers resent it when I do things differently from them at work.

☐ My employer doesn't agree with or support my professional goals.

☐ I don't feel as though I have a stake in the company I work for.

☐ Family members, friends, co-workers and employers have offered unsolicited advice about how to live my life.

☐ People have said hurtful things to me as if to "put me in my place."

☐ I have followed others' advice, even when I felt it wasn't right for me.

☐ Other: _____

### CLAIM IT!

☐ My family, friends, co-workers and/or employer are crabs in my bucket. I feel resistance from one or more of these groups when I do things in a way I know is healthy for me.

**Reflect On It** When your friends and family members pull you back down into your bucket, they're not necessarily trying to sabotage you. They're just functioning at a different frequency than the new you. It's not your place to judge them. Just wish them well on their own journeys, even if they don't include you. Then focus on your own goals and dreams, and move on!

# YOU

You might identify another one of the crabs in your bucket by simply looking in the mirror. Yes, while it might be difficult to accept, you might be giving away your personal power to other crabs without even realizing it! Believe me, the crabs that live in your head can be even more destructive than those in the outside world. Why? Because they disguise themselves as logic, truth and reality; they've been living in your psyche for a long time, and they're all too happy to have the run of the place. Take a moment to relax and set your self-awareness meter on "high." Then read through the checklist below and check the boxes next to the statements you recognize in yourself.

☐ I'm still not really sure what my personal boundaries are.

☐ It is challenging for me to maintain my boundaries when someone I love wants something that goes against my values.

☐ I let people get away with saying negative things to me or about me.

☐ I find it difficult to stand up for myself in the face of conflict.

☐ I have trouble taking responsibility for my detrimental financial choices and habits.

☐ I often have negative and self-defeating thoughts that tell me I'm not good enough or smart enough to reach my goals.

☐ It is a challenge for me to transform my negative thoughts into positive thoughts.

☐ I remember being told I would never be able to reach a goal or fulfill a dream and believing it was true.

☐ I define my value by what others think of me.

☐ Other people have projected their dissatisfaction with aspects of themselves onto me, and I have accepted their criticism as the truth.

☐ Other: _____

## CLAIM IT!

☐ I am one of the crabs in my bucket. My negative self-image is holding me back from expressing my Inner Wealth.

# CRABS IN YOUR BUCKET
## *The Emotion Behind Money* Exercise 16

Okay, folks, you know you've got 'em. Now it's time to list 'em—the crabs in your bucket. If you become aware of the people and obstacles that you allow to hold you back, your radar will be more likely to catch a crab in action. Review the checklists you've just completed. What specific crabs come to mind? Which crabs have had the strongest influence on your life?

I'll start you off with an example: My mom was a big crab while I was writing my book. Mom is a retired English teacher. Whenever I mentioned the project, she would remind me of all the nights she had stayed up with me when I had papers due for school and how grueling the process had been for her. I decided very quickly that the topic was off limits with my mom until the book was done.

Another example involves college. When as a seventeen-year-old I would talk about applying to Notre Dame, so many people told me, "People like us don't go to Notre Dame, Jul, we're just fans." Even my own father was a crab! He said, "Kids like you don't go to Notre Dame. We just don't have enough money." Unfortunately, at that age I listened to all these crabs, and I never even applied.

List your crabs in the left column of the chart on the opposite page. For each crab, record the messages you hear from it, literally and figuratively, in the center column. In the right column, describe the impact each crab has on your life. Does it keep you from speaking up for yourself? Does it keep you from following your dreams?

| CRAB | MESSAGE | IMPACT |
| --- | --- | --- |
|  |  |  |

# CRABS IN YOUR BUCKET
*(continued)*

**Process It** Once you've filled in the chart describing the crabs in your bucket, keep it handy and use it to deal with them in positive ways that are healthy for you. Pretty soon all of your pesky crabs will sidle off into oblivion!

If you expect to encounter one of your crabs, try to shift your thinking beforehand. Say to yourself: "I am a happy, healthy, intelligent person. I know what's right for me. There is nothing standing in the way of my ideal life."

See "Appendix A: Crabs in Your Bucket" on page 159 for an extra blank chart. Use it to keep track of the new crabs you encounter. When you meet one, describe it in the chart and intentionally choose how to respond to it.

# THE CRABS IN YOUR BUCKET:
# TYING IT ALL TOGETHER

Your personal growth might cause those close to you to examine their own lives, which may in turn make them uncomfortable, consciously or unconsciously. As you change, your friends and/or loved ones might respond to you like crabs in a bucket: when one tries to escape, the others all reach up with their claws to pull it back down.

Now that you've identified the crabs in your bucket, it's time to take back the personal power you've given to them. This is an important step in actualizing your ideal life. Don't underestimate, however, how difficult it can be when the people you love distance themselves from you once you choose to change. But I've always said that people come and go in our lives for good reasons. I promise you that any friend or family member whose approval or affection you might lose as a result of following your life's purpose will be replaced tenfold—if not in number, then in quality.

**Process It** Use the chart on the next page to help you imagine the process of climbing out of your bucket and beginning a life independent of the other crabs.

 In the bottom box, describe what life with the other crabs has been like for you. Allow yourself to recognize the painful aspects of giving away your power to others.

 Then visualize what it means to use your personal power in healthy ways, for your own benefit. Picture the specific ways in which your life will change when you leave the other crabs behind. Imagine it in Technicolor, down to the smallest detail. In the top boxes of the chart, describe three ways your life will change. Choose the three examples that feel the most powerful to you.

 When completing the chart, use whatever form of expression that feels authentic to you, whether that means writing a narrative or drawing pictures or simply listing phrases or adjectives.

Removing the crabs from your life means creating the space for the new you!

# THE CRABS IN YOUR BUCKETS:
## TYING IT ALL TOGEHER
*(continued)*

### CLIMBING OUT OF THE BUCKET

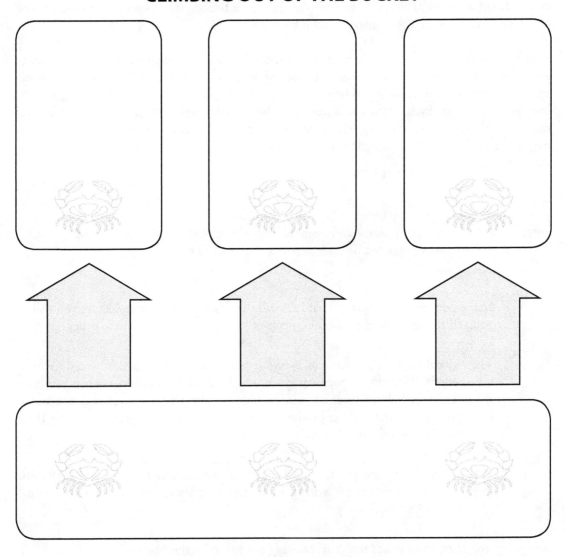

7

# FACING YOUR FINANCIAL REALITY

*"If you do what you've always done, you'll
get what you've always gotten."*

—Tony Robbins

# LIFE RESPONSIBILITIES EXERCISE

*The Emotion Behind Money* Exercise 17

Most of us were taught at a very young age to judge ourselves, to see our behavior as good or bad, right or wrong. But self-judgment only stirs the pot of guilt, an emotion that is not useful in building the life you want.

The next step toward financial healing is to set guilt and other emotions aside and to look at your life objectively—your responsibilities and realities, the good and the bad. Think about the four aspects of the Life Navigation Wheel: work life, family life, personal life and financial life. On the pages that follow, jot down what each area looks like in the present tense. Try to see your life as though you are on the outside studying yourself, gathering facts and information. When you feel yourself beginning to label some aspect of your life "good" or "bad," remember that your mission is to collect facts. All that's required at this juncture is objectivity.

Accept your particular responsibilities: you might have kids, a job, parents, bills, a spouse, friends. Acknowledge what you don't like about your life. Maybe you don't like your physical body; maybe you don't like your work. If you know that your company favors younger, cheaper labor and that your quick rise to the top has ended, write it down without begrudging the point. If your spouse has a difficult time holding onto money, put that down as a statement, not a judgment. If you have all three of your children's college funds in order, write it down.

Look at each aspect of your life and recognize it for what it is. Try it! It's very empowering! But remember, no judging!

## YOUR WORK LIFE
(work, continuing education, professional development)

What does your work life look like right now? Are you expected to work overtime, or do you sometimes find yourself with nothing to do? Do you feel as though your job is your vocation, or is it just a job? Be as honest, straightforward and objective as you can in describing what your work life looks like in the present moment.

# LIFE RESPONSIBILITIES EXERCISE
### *(continued)*

## YOUR FAMILY LIFE
(spouse, children, parents, siblings, home life)

Is your current family life calm, chaotic or confusing? Are you single, engaged, married with children? Do you have young children who need daily care or children in college? What are your roles and responsibilities when it comes to family? Are you a stay-at-home parent or a main breadwinner? Describe the realities of your family life at this moment in time.

# YOUR PERSONAL LIFE
(interests, hobbies, friendships, self-improvement)

What interests do you have that benefit you and only you? Are you a voracious reader, or do you find you're too tired at the end of the day to pick up a book? Are you a homebody, or do you travel every chance you get? Do you find yourself bored when you have unexpected free time, or does there never seem to be enough time to pursue your favorite friendships or hobbies? What does your personal life look like right now?

# LIFE RESPONSIBILITIES EXERCISE
*(continued)*

## YOUR FINANCIAL LIFE
(money, possessions, investments)

How would you describe the current state of your financial life? Do you have a lot of money saved? Have you accrued a large amount of debt over the years? What do your spending habits look like when you view them objectively? Remember, your answers reflect the current state of your financial affairs, which is separate from your worth as a person!

**Process It** From time to time, refer to the lists you just made. They can be a great reminder of the facts without letting any damaging emotions get in the way. Remember, judging yourself accomplishes nothing. There are enough people in the world who will do that for us. When you're true to yourself and not listening to everyone else, you retain your personal power, and you're free to be the honest author of your own life, the pitch-perfect conductor of your own symphony!

 Which aspect of your life was easiest for you to view objectively?

_____

 Why do you think it is easiest for you to distance yourself emotionally from that particular aspect of your life? For example, if you find it easiest to view your work life objectively, is it because you have spent time thinking about and applying your strengths when it comes to your profession? If you're able to view your family life most objectively, is it because you understand that some parts of family life—such as what your parents decide to do with their retirement or what your in-laws think of you—are out of your control?

_____

_____

_____

_____

 Do you see how freeing it is to look at an aspect of your life without getting tangled up in self-judgment and self-blame? Now use your talent for seeing this one aspect of your life clearly, and apply it to the other aspects of your life. Return to your lists on the previous pages and add any details that come to light in your more objective frame of mind.

# YOUR FINANCIAL DARK SIDE
## *EBM* Exercise 18

We all have a shadow or dark side in some aspect of our lives. This is the side of you that flies in the face of compassion and open-mindedness and sometimes even sinks into bigotry. It's often fear-based and almost always a great distorter of truths. Your relationship with money, like mine, has a dark side, and it feeds on negativity. It's the source of all unhealthy financial behavior.

Take a few moments now to relax and cast your mind back on all the work you've done so far on letting your Inner Wealth guide your life decisions. From that viewpoint, allow yourself to recognize the dark underbelly of your relationship with money. Think about the ways you use money. Do you spend it to soothe inner pain? Think about your beliefs about money. Do you, deep down, believe that money can buy you happiness? Think about your feelings about money. Do you have negative feelings about people who have money, or on the flipside, people who don't have a lot of money? What feelings, fears, joys or emotional agitations are hiding behind your financial personality? These behaviors, beliefs and feelings are neither right nor wrong; they just are.

Whenever you're ready, describe the negative behaviors, beliefs and feelings you've associated with money. To help you get started, here is a list I made of my dark-side beliefs about money:

1. Money buys love.
2. Money buys freedom.
3. Money makes you happy.
4. People with excess money are not good people.
5. Money validates your character.
6. Money is the only meaning of success.

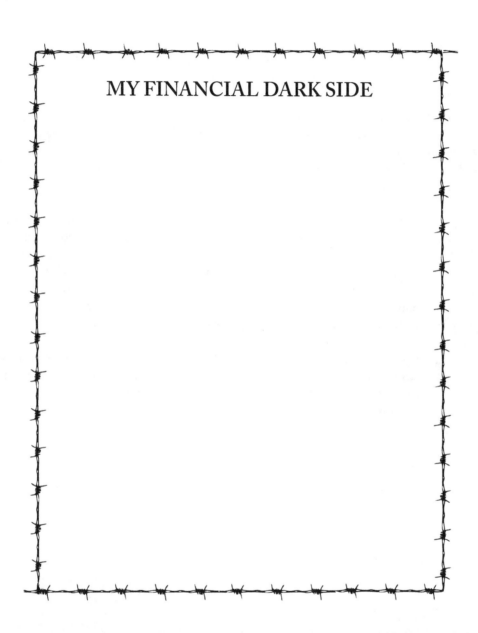

## MY FINANCIAL DARK SIDE

**Reflect On It** Looking at how the dark or shadow side of money is manifesting in your life will set you on the path to mastering your financial behavior and achieving financial freedom. Having your financial dark side cracked wide open can make you feel vulnerable and possibly a little ashamed of yourself, but it's also extremely empowering.

# YOUR FINANCIAL DARK SIDE
*(continued)*

After I made my list of all the lies I told myself about money, I still didn't feel free. My friend Anne Emerson, a gifted healer, explained to me that as children, in an attempt to escape pain, we subconsciously bury hurtful experiences and events and the emotions they stir up. It's painful for us as adults to bring these memories to the surface. However, Anne explained, if I wanted to heal my dark side, I would have to confront its origin.

Anne helped me recall a memory from second grade that shone a bright light on a particular financial behavior of mine: my excessive generosity with gifts. My second-grade teacher, Mrs. Clark, had scolded me for talking, and I decided I would win back her approval by buying her the most expensive Christmas gift I could afford. When this memory came back to me, I realized that as an eight-year-old I had forged a financial pattern of giving expensive gifts—a pattern I was still following many years later. I gave these gifts not only because I was and am a very giving person but also because, deep down, I was seeking love and approval.

Review the description of your financial dark side that you wrote on the previous page. What memories come to mind? Grab the first association or flash of memory that occurs to you, however vague it might seem at first, and write a description of it in the space on the opposite page. What conclusions can you draw about the memory and its meaning when it comes to your current financial behavior? What pattern does it highlight?

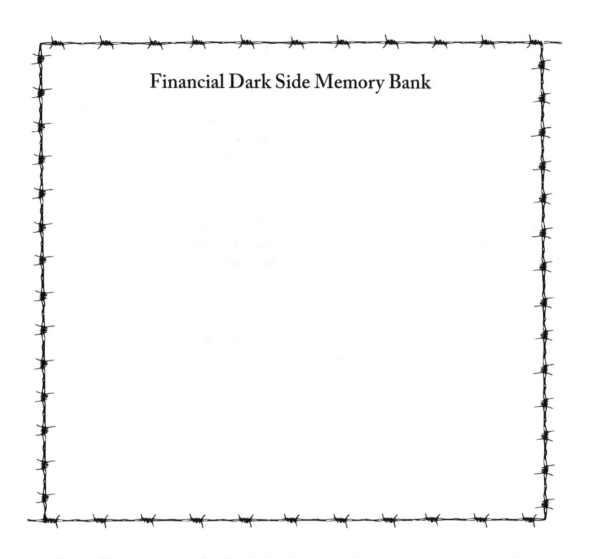

## Financial Dark Side Memory Bank

**Reflect On It**  I've always believed that once something emerges from your subconscious, you can never put it back. I made a commitment to myself that regardless of what emotions emerged, especially my fears of rejection and not being loved, rather than act on them, I would sit with them and let them pass through my psyche and my body until they dissipated and I could move past them. It was a very difficult emotional process, believe me. And don't get me wrong, I still have urges to act out when I fear rejection or catch myself trying to force someone to love me. For the most part, though, I'm pretty confident that I've dealt consciously with my dark side, at least with my shadow relationship with money. Now it's your turn.

# YOUR FINANCIAL KARMA

The Hindu concept of karma is that every day we make choices that create consequences. As a result, each day we face the consequences of our past decisions, every single one of them, good and bad. We are the sum of those decisions. For example, if you have a lot of debt or a lack of savings, it's typically because you made a choice to spend more than your income, or you didn't pay yourself first by putting some money into savings.

The good news is that the choices that you've made in the past don't define your future; your future is defined by what you do today. Here's an example of what I mean: My body used to be overweight because of the food choices I'd made. Then I chose to only eat foods that fueled my body, and that became my new reality, even while my body was still overweight. Those behaviors in the present moment created a different reality in my future, which is the body that I have today. Show me what you're doing today, and I'll tell you what your future holds.

**?** Give some examples of how past choices, in any aspect of your life, have made you happier in the present moment.

What small, specific choices can you make in your financial realm today that will define a more positive future for you?

_____

_____

_____

_____

_____

_____

**Reflect On It** Live in the present. There's no other time like it. If you choose to live with positive intentions for what you want tomorrow, and you position yourself to be lucky, you stand a much better chance of getting what you want than if you did nothing at all.

# FACING YOUR FINANCIAL REALITY: TYING IT ALL TOGETHER

It's important to understand and acknowledge your responsibilities in life without judgment. They are the outcome of decisions you've made in the past. You cannot change the past. You can only change your behavior in the present moment, which will create your new future. Learn to live in the present with positive intentions for your money, and you'll set yourself up for success.

Think objectively about the decisions you've made to create your present financial reality. In the left column of the chart below, list some of the financial decisions that have brought negative consequences in your present life. In the right column, describe the consequences.

| PAST DECISIONS | NEGATIVE CONSEQUENCES |
|---|---|
| | |

Now, using the same objective lens, list your present financial intentions and describe the success they will bring in the future.

| PRESENT INTENTIONS | FUTURE SUCCESS |
| --- | --- |
|  |  |

# SECTION THREE
Financial Transformation

8

# SETTING YOUR INTENTIONS

*"All our dreams can come true, if we have
the courage to pursue them."*

—Walt Disney

# MAKE ROOM FOR ABUNDANCE

*The Emotion Behind Money* **Exercise 19**

When I decided to clean out my closets in 2006, my goal was to give away one bag of clothes a month for a year. Every month, I filled a giant sack and took it to the Salvation Army. It felt so good to see that physical space open up that by the end of the year, I'd given away thirty-six bags of clothing. At the same time, it wasn't easy to part with some of these clothes, especially the items that had sentimental value.

Your money works the same way. If you want something other than what you have today, you need to make space for it. Having one fewer latte during the week makes space for that savings account to grow. When you make space, you allow the flow of money to start.

Take a moment to think about what you could remove from your current life to make room for your new life. Go back and revisit the Life Navigation Wheel that you created for the Life Transformation exercise in chapter 5, page 75. Looking at your ideal life, make a list of what you could do to make room for those things to occur. Ask yourself, "What in my life right now doesn't support my dreams?" It could be anything from the food in your fridge to the clothes in your closet, your job, your house or your personal prejudices. It could be the magazines you have lying around that tempt you to buy unnecessary stuff. It could be pictures of old friends or ex-boyfriends or girlfriends. You have to physically move out the old to make room for the new!

Don't limit it to material things—it could also be people. Which friends are really not supporting you in your desire to change and move forward? In the space on the opposite page, write down everything you can think of. No one else will see your list, so don't hold back.

**Process It** When you've finished making your list, read through it. Circle at least one thing and commit right now to removing it from your life. Trust me, you'll find it most rewarding.

# DIRECTING YOUR MONEY FLOW

For the next few minutes, I want you to forget everything you've ever learned about cash flow. I don't even want you to think about money as dollar bills, coins, checks, credit cards or account balances. Instead, I want you to think of money as a form of energy. It's an energy that flows through your life. It can be positive energy, or it can be negative energy. Sit for a few moments and imagine it flowing. Now that you're in this frame of mind, consider the following questions as they apply to your money energy:

? Where do you focus your financial energy?

_____

_____

? Do you dwell on how little you have or how to acquire more? If so, what form do those thoughts take?

_____

_____

_____

? How do you nourish your energy?

_____

_____

_____

? What do you think you're doing that might slow or block the flow of energy?

_____

_____

_____

What or who around you drains your energy? List as many examples as you can, and explain how they drain you. Remember, no one will see this list but you.

_____

_____

_____

Do you ever store your energy for use at a later date, or do you burn it continuously?

_____

_____

_____

**Process It** Now apply the energy metaphor to the literal money in your life. Picture yourself writing a check to pay toward a big credit card bill. I bet you feel the energy draining right out of your toes, don't you?

What does your cash flow feel like on an energetic level? Does it serve a purpose, or is it a rambling stream, wandering here and there? Remember, how much you make isn't as important as what you do with it once it comes in. If you're a planner, you might direct a large chunk of cash toward your retirement. If you're a spender or a giver, perhaps every dime of your income goes toward eating out, entertaining friends or buying gifts for yourself and for others. Describe how your cash flow feels to you right now.

_____

_____

_____

_____

_____

# YOUR MONEY INTENTIONS
## *EBM* Exercise 20

If you have cash coming in the door, you must ask yourself what your personal strategy is. What do you want that money to do for you? What are you drawn to? What is true for you first and foremost? What is your heart's desire? Think about these questions in terms of your intentions for three timelines: the short-term, mid-term and long-term.

The intentions you set with your money are extremely powerful. Creating an intention is a spiritual process that links our desires to the physical world. Isn't it remarkable that something so life-changing can be so easy? All you have to do is want something and then live as if it's already yours.

In order to make your intentions real, you need to refer once more to the Life Navigation Wheel you completed for the Life Transformation exercise in chapter 5, page 75. If you choose to live the life you've envisioned, you must set financial intentions to get there. We're going to start where you're comfortable. It doesn't matter if your first intention is big or small; just be where you are now emotionally. Imagine that achieving your dreams is like building a four-foot model of the Statue of Liberty out of Legos: you have to start with just one humble little block. You're going to spread your dreams out on the floor and look at them. Then choose one step to begin with in the process of building your new life.

Take a look at the dream life you described on your Life Navigation Wheel on page 75. Choose just one detail right now to focus on. It can be from any of the four areas: work, family, personal or financial. What feels like the right detail to begin with? What resonates with you right now? Do you have any regrets in your life that you'd like to remedy? Is there anything that makes you feel at war with yourself, a fight between your heart and your mind?

In the space below, write the detail you've chosen. Then make a list of what you could do financially to achieve it. It might be changing how you spend or saving a certain amount of cash each month. It might be researching a new career or breaking up with a boyfriend or girlfriend who drains your reserves financially and emotionally. Let loose! List everything you can think of.

# YOUR MONEY INTENTIONS
### *(continued)*

**Process It** Writing down your intentions is the step between just thinking about doing something and actually taking the steps necessary in the real world to make your dream come true.

 When you feel you're ready, read back over the list you made on the previous page. Select the two actions from the list that excite you the most. Try to ignore how big or small they seem or how easy or difficult they will be for you to master. Just use them to complete the sentences below. As you fill in the blanks, picture yourself living the life you created by making each of these dreams come true. Feel the excitement, the joy and the gratitude as if you have already realized your dreams.

In order to reach my dream of _____ ,

I will _____ .



I choose to _____

in order to manifest my life's desire of _____ .

 As you begin to change your life one step at a time, use sentences like these as stepping stones between thought and action. Write a sentence like this each time you feel you're ready to take an item from a list on your Life Navigation Wheel and make it real.

 In addition to writing down your intentions, I invite you to make signs or cut out images that depict your new life. Put them where you can see them daily. Make a collage you can hang up. Honor your intentions; revere them. They are your golden ticket to nirvana. Treat them like the precious gems they are.

If your self-talk is something other than positive, change it! Your inner touchstone, your positive inner voice, your intuition can guide you better than anything else out there in the external world. If you feel like you're tied down in life, say to yourself every day, "I am free," and you will begin to feel free.

Think of a positive message about what you want your money to do for you. You can think of it as a statement, a mantra or anything else—that doesn't matter. Its purpose is to assist you in manifesting your ideal world. It could be something like "Money will abundantly flow to me with immediacy and ease." Feel free to create more than one and to add to and change these messages as time goes on.

_____

_____

_____

_____

 Oddly enough, sometimes it's difficult to stay open and allow yourself to receive abundance, particularly when it's exactly what you want. I don't know about you, but I wasn't raised that way, and I found myself doing things that blocked my best intentions. Once you begin to manifest what you want in your life, make sure to continue to repeat your intentions each day. Also, when you get what you've always wanted, be sure to say, "Thank you! More, please!"

**Reflect On It** Your inner voice, that self-talk that forms your spirit, can either free you or hold you down. Which do you choose? You have to believe you deserve your ideal life. The minute you start to listen to those crabs of doubt, they pull you down and become your reality.

# BE CAREFUL WHAT YOU WISH FOR

There's a Bible saying that goes like this: "You reap what you sow." The law of attraction works both ways. The same way you can attract what you want, you can also attract what you don't want by giving energy to the negative circumstances and behavior that might exist around you. I have a family member who complained often about her spouse's inadequacies. I suggested, "Why not try to find the things you really appreciate and reward the behavior you want?" She started finding things she could thank her husband for, and, lo and behold, he began to deliver these things more and more frequently. As a result, she was also able to recognize the self-fulfilling prophecy she had created by focusing on the negative in her marriage. What are you doing that's clipping your wings and preventing you from soaring in your life?

Take a few moments right now to identify anything that's been nagging at you lately, circumstances that cast a shadow of negativity over any aspect of your life. List as many of these things as you can think of in as much detail as you can.

_____

_____

_____

_____

_____

_____

_____

_____

_____

_____

_____

_____

Now choose one topic from your list and describe as many positive things you can think of about this same topic, no matter how small or trivial they may seem. Isn't it amazing how many positive things you notice when you set your mind to it, even about something you thought of before as overwhelmingly negative?

_____

_____

_____

_____

_____

_____

_____

_____

_____

**Reflect On It** It's important to be persistent. Circumstances and behaviors may not shift immediately. There is no instant gratification here, which I know is tough for many of us in the Western world to accept, but be patient. It's like working out at the gym: You need to build up your muscles day by day. It takes time.

# WHAT'S IN YOUR BUCKET?

Successful wealth-building relies on setting intentions for your income in three different segments or buckets: short-term, mid-term and long-term. In order to fund them with your intentions, you first have to know how they're set up to work for you.

## Short - Term
(1 year money)

Saving Accounts
(3-6 months in
emergency reserves)
Online Savings Accounts
Certificates of Deposit
(CD's)
Money Market

## Mid - Term
(2-10 year money)

Stocks
Bonds
Mutual Funds
Real Estate Investment
Limited Partnerships

## Long - Term
(10+ year money)

Employer Retirement Plan
ROTH IRA
Cash Value Life Insurance
Annuities
After Tax IRA

Take a minute and think about your current cash flow as it relates to the short-term, mid-term and long-term buckets. Be as objective about and accepting of your current reality as you can. The purpose isn't to judge but rather to raise your awareness of where your money flows. Fill in the blanks and check the boxes next to whatever is true in your financial reality right now.

# SHORT-TERM BUCKET
(one year)

The current balance in my short-term bucket is $_____.

I am funding my short-term bucket by $_____ each (circle one)
week / paycheck / month / quarter / year.

☐ Yes ☐ No   I am comfortable with the amount of money I have in emergency reserves.
☐ Yes ☐ No   I refuse to use my credit card as my emergency reserve.
☐ Yes ☐ No   I set money aside for monthly and annual bills.
☐ Yes ☐ No   I have money invested in CDs.
☐ Yes ☐ No   I have money invested in a money market account.
☐ Yes ☐ No   I feel secure emotionally about my short-term bucket.
☐ Yes ☐ No   I am married or partnered.
☐ Yes ☐ No   If yes, my partner and I are in harmony about our intentions for our short-term bucket.

In your ideal world, what would your short-term bucket look like? How much cash would you have in the bank in case of an emergency? How much money would you put toward short-term investments? Would you like to pay down your debt considerably? Do you want to begin an autopilot saving plan? Do you want to harmonize your short-term goals with those of your spouse? What intentions can you set right now for the next year—both in your financial life and in any other areas of your life?

# WHAT'S IN YOUR BUCKET?

*(continued)*

## MID-TERM BUCKET
(two to ten years)

The current balance in my mid-term bucket is $_____.

I am funding my mid-term bucket by $_____ each (circle one)
week / paycheck / month / quarter / year.

☐ Yes ☐ No  I have money invested in stocks, bonds and/or mutual funds.

☐ Yes ☐ No  I am saving money for higher education for myself or my family members.

☐ Yes ☐ No  If yes, I am using a 529 Plan for college planning.

☐ Yes ☐ No  I own real estate (other than my own home) or have money invested in real estate through a limited partnership, limited liability corporation or real estate investment trust.

☐ Yes ☐ No  I feel secure emotionally about my mid-term bucket.

☐ Yes ☐ No  I am married or partnered.

☐ Yes ☐ No  If yes, my partner and I are in harmony about our intentions for our mid-term bucket.

In your ideal world, what would your mid-term bucket look like? What intentions would you like to set for the next two to ten years in your financial life and in the other aspects of your life? Do you want a new home? Are you yearning for a new car? Is your family life what you want it to be? Do you want to move to a warmer climate? Do you want to retire? Shift careers? Have a child? Once you know where you want to go, you can align your money to support your dreams and desires.

_____

_____

# LONG-TERM BUCKET
(ten years plus)

The current balance in my long-term bucket is $_____.

I am funding my long-term bucket by $_____ each (circle one)
week / paycheck / month / quarter / year.

☐ Yes  ☐ No  I have a 401(k), 403(b), 457 plan or other employer retirement plan.

☐ Yes  ☐ No  My employer has a matching program for retirement.

☐ Yes  ☐ No  If yes, I take full advantage of my employer's matching program.

☐ Yes  ☐ No  I have money invested in a Roth IRA or after-tax IRA.

☐ Yes  ☐ No  I have money invested in annuities.

☐ Yes  ☐ No  I feel secure emotionally about my long-term bucket.

☐ Yes  ☐ No  I am married or partnered.

☐ Yes  ☐ No  If yes, my partner and I are in harmony about our intentions for our long-term bucket.

In your ideal world, what would your long-term bucket look like? What intentions would you like to set for ten or more years in the future? Do you have your heart set on a particular career trajectory? Do you want to work part-time at some point in your life in order to travel or follow other dreams and desires? How do you envision your semi-retired or retired years?

_____

_____

_____

**Reflect On It**  Your current balances are the fulfillment of your financial karma—the result of the past choices you have made. The amount of money you have in any account, fund or policy never has been and never will be the result of some magical, mystical process. Now that you have a sense of what you want out of life, you can use your personal power to get to your ideal.

# LIFE PHASES EXERCISE

New clients always ask me to advise them about how much they should have in each bucket. I believe there are no generic *shoulds* to building wealth. How you apportion your flow of wealth depends on your core values, on your personal goals and dreams, on the way you feel about money and on your phase of life. The primary consideration for most people is the phase of life. Your intentions about money change as you move from your twenties to your thirties, and your financial considerations are certainly different at sixty than they were at forty. Turn to Appendix B and complete the section of the Life Phases Worksheet for your phase of life. Then answer the questions below.

I am in my (circle one) twenties / thirties / forties / fifties / sixties / seventies / eighties.

How secure do you feel in your present stage of life? What do you feel are your strongest areas? What areas of your life phase do you need to strengthen?

_____

_____

_____

_____

_____

What specific intentions can you set to address the areas of your life phase that need strengthening?

_____

_____

_____

_____

Are you wrestling with thoughts of success and failure? For example, do you find yourself changing your mind about a dream or goal for fear you might not succeed? Describe that struggle.

What is the biggest obstacle to having the life you desire?

What kind of financial karma are you creating right now? What kind of financial karma would you like to start creating?

What aspects of your life do you want to energize with additional cash flow?

# SETTING YOUR INTENTIONS:
# TYING IT ALL TOGETHER

Transforming your current life into the one you truly desire doesn't happen overnight. You have to break the process down into digestible, bite-sized pieces. Financial healing occurs both internally through your emotions and externally through your day-to-day behavior. You can begin to reshape your behavior by redirecting your cash flow and by utilizing the power of intent. In the chart below, describe in as much detail as possible two small changes you intend to make in your spending habits that represent the first steps toward the life of your dreams.

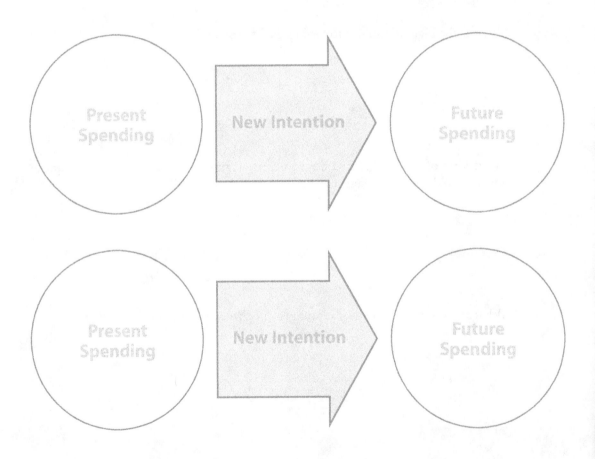

# LIVES THAT THRIVE

*"Doing what you love is the cornerstone of having abundance in your life."*

—Wayne Dyer

# INTERGRATING INNER WEALTH

I believe the best way for you to understand financial healing is to see how others have integrated their Inner Wealth into their financial lives. Review the descriptions of Nick and Katrina, Jack and Diane, and Carl and Ann in chapter 9 of *The Emotion Behind Money*. These couples exemplify some of the issues I've found in the Early Accumulation, Later Accumulation and Distribution phases of life, which are roughly equivalent to young adulthood, middle age and retirement.

From the description of each couple, pull out the details you find most compelling. Which issues remind you of your own? Which strategies appeal to you as you begin to live your Inner Wealth? For each couple, check the boxes next to the details that feel true to you. Then describe the ways in which each couple's situation is relevant to your past, present or future, regardless of which life phase you're in.

## EARLY ACCUMULATION PHASE: NICK AND KATRINA

☐ I want to leave behind my debt and the shame I associate with it.

☐ I want to take the time to discover what my dream job really is.

☐ When I have children, I want to be able to support their dreams and goals financially.

☐ I'm excited at the prospect of living out my personal dreams, but I'm not quite sure how to begin.

☐ I want to make sure living my Inner Wealth will be compatible with my partner's goals and dreams.

☐ Other _____

Describe how Nick and Katrina's situation is  relevant to yours. What good ideas can you take from their story and apply to your own life? If you're already beyond the Early Accumulation Phase, what memories did reading Nick and Katrina's story bring up for you?

_____

_____

_____

_____

_____

_____

## LATER ACCUMULATION PHASE: JACK AND DIANE

☐ I worry about my financial future.

☐ I know what my dream job is, and I want to finally make it a reality.

☐ I want to support my parents and help my children with expenses like college and weddings.

☐ It's been difficult for me to get back in touch with my personal dreams.

☐ After focusing on caring for others for years, my partner and I need to redefine our purposes in life.

☐ Other _____

Describe how Jack and Diane's situation is relevant to yours. What good ideas can you take from their story and apply to your own life? If you're not currently in the Later Accumulation Phase, what connections can you make between Jack and Diane's story and your memories of the past or dreams of the future?

_____

_____

_____

_____

_____

# INTEGRATING INNER WEALTH

*(continued)*

## DISTRIBUTION PHASE: CARL AND ANN

☐ I feel financially secure and prepared for retirement.

☐ I haven't really thought about what I want to do with my time after I'm retired.

☐ I want to make sure my parents are provided for in their old age.

☐ My life reflects my personal interests, whether through my home décor, my garden or another hobby or activity.

☐ Other _____

? Describe how Carl and Ann's situation is relevant to yours. What good ideas can you take from their story and apply to your own life? If you have not yet reached the Distribution Phase, explore what Carl and Ann's story makes you think about your own future.

_____

_____

_____

_____

_____

_____

_____

_____

Now think about your Inner Wealth and how it manifests itself. In what specific ways, small and large, does your Inner Wealth shine in your life? How have you integrated it into the work, family and personal aspects of your life? No detail is too small to include here.

# INTERGRATING INNER WEALTH

### *(continued)*

In what ways do you recognize the Inner Wealth of people close to you? How do they manifest their Inner Wealth in their everyday lives? What examples of attitudes, habits and behaviors do you see in them that you would like to use as an example when you set intentions for your own life?

# LIVES THAT THRIVE:
# TYING IT ALL TOGETHER

In each phase of our lives, we must adjust our financial behavior to the particular characteristics of that phase. In the Early Accumulation phase (roughly equivalent to young adulthood), couples should consciously decide how they want to merge their money. During the Later Accumulation phase (middle age), many people fulfill their financial obligations to their parents and their children, and find themselves with higher taxes but also more money to save and invest. In the Distribution phase (retirement age), people often have to learn how to dream again.

Whichever phase of life you happen to be in, integrating your soul's purpose with the other aspects of your life can have only one result: making your dreams come true! Use the space below to describe your phase of life—Early Accumulation, Later Accumulation or Distribution—and to set some personal intentions for making your dreams and desires your reality.

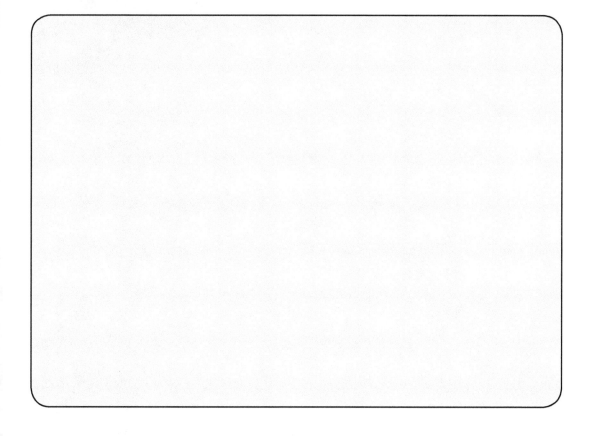

# BUILDING AND RENOVATING
# YOUR PORTFOLIO

*"Action is the foundational
key to all success."*

—Pablo Picasso

# YOUR PERSONAL STRATEGY

The majority of financial services professionals approach banking, risk-management and investing as a black-and-white, logical discipline. Their minds function predominantly in the realms of logic, analysis and rational thought. In other words, they are left-brainers. While many of them are whip-smart, their priorities do not match their clients'. Most financial services clients are right-brain thinkers who tend to look at life more holistically, subjectively and, yes, emotionally.

Let's look at the two pyramids below that illustrate how this dynamic between financial services professionals and their clients is often misaligned. In the Product Motivated Relationship, illustrated by the pyramid on the left, the client's personal strategy is allowed only the smallest portion of the pyramid, while financial products create the largest portion. Many financial services professionals start the process with the products they have to offer, rather than with an attempt to understand their clients' dreams, goals or priorities. I find this approach backward and unstable.

In the model of the Client Advocacy Relationship on the right, the largest section of the pyramid is the client's personal strategy. This strategy creates a solid base for the other sections, which contain investment and insurance portfolios and financial products.

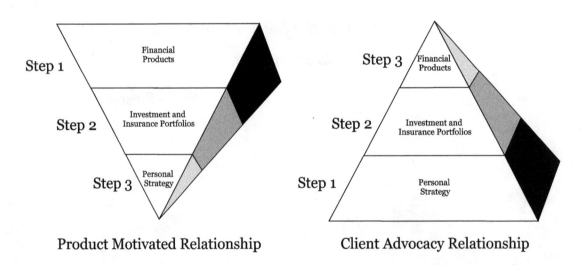

Product Motivated Relationship        Client Advocacy Relationship

The Product Driven Relationship is not only limiting for you, it begins with the wrong motivation. It would be like going to your favorite department store and seeing only flaming red, size 18 dresses on the rack and buying one even though you're a size 8 and look fabulous in navy blue. You absolutely cannot build a foundation for financial success when you start with a product, let alone a limited selection of products. You build wealth by defining your personal strategy, looking at the investments and insurance that you already have and determining if they support your personal strategy and are right for *you*.

The first step toward aligning your personal goals and dreams with the contents of your portfolio is to create a strategy based on you as an individual, you and your partner, and/or you and your immediate family. Your personal strategy guides your approach to your life right now. It takes into account your dreams, aspirations and goals. Answer the following questions to help define your personal strategy.

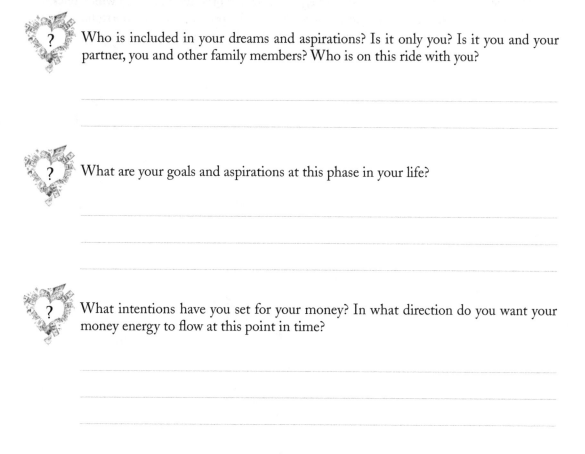

Who is included in your dreams and aspirations? Is it only you? Is it you and your partner, you and other family members? Who is on this ride with you?

What are your goals and aspirations at this phase in your life?

What intentions have you set for your money? In what direction do you want your money energy to flow at this point in time?

# YOUR PORTFOLIO
*The Emotion Behind Money* **Exercise 21**

Once you have created your personal strategy, the next step is to analyze your portfolio and compare it to that strategy. So, what's in your portfolio? It's time for you to get in there, take it apart and see. Go through all of your folders, statements and policies and put them in their respective buckets. Use the chart on the next page to categorize your investments and insurance policies as short-term, mid-term or long-term. Even if you don't know why you have that term life insurance or aren't sure where it goes, take your best guess. Remember, it's all tied to timelines.

**Reflect On It** Everyone has a different threshold when it comes to understanding finances and financial products. You may instinctively know which products belong in which bucket, or you may not have a clue. You should take a look at the products in your portfolio and try to make sense of them to the level that you're comfortable with. Do the best you can.

| SHORT-TERM | MID-TERM | LONG-TERM |
| --- | --- | --- |
|  |  |  |

# SHOPPING FOR A TRUSTED ADVISOR

The last step toward financial abundance is to select the financial products that are best suited to your goals and aspirations, products that complement or replace those in your current portfolio. Part of that process for most people includes finding a financial services professional who will work with you and for you rather than treating you as a vehicle for making money. Finding the right partner or client advocate to help you achieve your dreams is essential to success and happiness. I suggest you approach it as you would any relationship in which trust is key. Meet a lot of people, ask a lot of questions and get references!

In my opinion, you want a financial planner whose services are fee-based rather than commission-based. This way, the more money you make, the more money your advisor makes, whether he or she is called a broker, planner, advisor or vice president. Fee-based advisors are also likely to be compensated to support a client advocacy relationship. They are paid by a company, bank or investment firm that promotes ongoing service. As such, they are highly motivated financially to be your advocate. They have time to explore your personality and emotions in addition to your financial reality.

Consider the list of questions on the following pages as you shop for a trusted advisor. Take these questions with you during your initial consultation. You'll find three blank worksheets containing these questions in Appendix C at the back of this workbook.

## QUESTIONS FOR FINANCIAL SERVICES PROFESSIONALS

- Is your income fee-based or commission-based?

- What designations do you have? [I suggest looking for a Certified Financial Planner or CFP®.]

- Are you tied to any sales goals with specific products?

- Are you working with any vendors who require you to sell a minimum number of their products or your contract with them will end? [Meaning, do you have any quotas you must reach?]

- What are your limitations, if any, in selling specific product lines due to your current licensing? [Someone who is fully licensed has a Series 7 and Series 66 to be fee-based.]

- Do you charge an annual planning fee outside of compensation from products? If you don't, why not?

- [If you're talking to an independent planner] If something were to happen to you, who will take care of me?

- [If you're talking to someone associated with a firm] What happens if you leave the business by choice, disability or death? Who would then be managing my money?

# SHOPPING FOR A TRUSTED ADVISOR

*(continued)*

After your initial consultation, complete the "Questions to Ask Yourself" portion of the worksheet in Appendix C. Ask yourself if you think the financial services professional you're considering has the capacity to understand your emotion behind money. Does this person seem belittling in any way? Will he or she be able to shift your funds to your best advantage as your reality and dreams change? Does this person display the following qualities?

- Empathy
- Passion
- Conviction
- Tough love
- Clarity

**Process It** In addition to finding a trusted advisor to guide you, it's helpful to create your own "board of directors." Who among your friends, family members and professional mentors has your best interests at heart? Which of them can you count on to tell it like it is, should you fall back into unhealthy patterns of behavior? Think of people you admire and respect, people who would never in a million years make you feel ashamed.

 Make a list of these people. Give them permission to say, "Don't do that. It will keep you from getting where you want to be, my friend." Whenever the need arises, look at this list and choose a person you can reach out to who you know will understand without judging. Think of them as lighthouses. When storms come rolling in, as storms always will, you'll have them as beams of light to lead you to safety.

 Don't forget to say, "Thank you. More, please." Gratitude expressed to the people who help you and to the universe goes a long way.

# BUILDING AND RENOVATING YOUR PORTFOLIO: TYING IT ALL TOGETHER

The contents of your portfolio should be aligned with the person you have come to know a little better while reading this book—you! You have worked in this chapter to define your personal financial strategy and to compare it with your current financial products. Now it's time to find a trusted advisor to help you create a portfolio that reflects who you are as an individual, a professional who will help you manifest your financial intentions in the world.

 Review the chart you completed on page 151. How comfortable did you feel categorizing and learning more about your current financial products? Circle a number on the graph.

| 1 | 2 | 3 | 4 | 5 |
|---|---|---|---|---|

| very uncomfortable | | somewhat comfortable | | completely comfortable |

? If you circled a 1, 2 or 3 on the scale, what do you think would make you feel more comfortable as you build or revise your portfolio?

_____

_____

_____

_____

_____

# BUILDNG AND RENOVATING YOUR PORTFOLIO: TYING IT ALL TOGETHER

*(continued)*

If you've decided to work with a trusted advisor, what approach would you like to see in such a professional?" Choose any that apply from the checklists below.

☐ I do not want to work with a trusted advisor.

☐ I do want to work with a trusted advisor.

I want a trusted advisor who . . .

☐ can explain products clearly and thoroughly so I don't have to read too much.

☐ offers a few appropriate choices rather than overwhelming me with options.

☐ will summarize products and then give me plenty of reading materials to consider.

☐ will guide me as I do my own product research.

☐ is willing to discuss and give advice on products I've chosen independently.

☐ Other _____

If you've decided to work with a trusted advisor, which financial services professionals do you plan to contact for initial consultations? Where did you get their names? Why are you considering them for the role of trusted advisor? Make a list here.

_____

_____

_____

_____

_____

# BENEDICITON

By now you are able to see how your finances and your life's purpose are woven tightly together by your intentions. My hope is that the exercises and processes in this book and workbook have allowed you to hear what your inner voice is trying to tell you. Listen to what it's saying. The answers are not always immediately clear, but just the fact that you're asking questions of your life opens your future to a myriad of exciting possibilities and positive change. We all want more out of life. We all want more than our reality currently offers. But abundance isn't just money. Follow your life's purpose and passion, my friend, and you will have it all, and the money will follow!

Thank you for taking this journey with me!

# APPENDIX A: CRABS IN YOUR BUCKET

| CRAB | MESSAGE | IMPACT |
|------|---------|--------|
|      |         |        |

# APPENDIX B: LIFE PHASES WORKSHEET

Here are the top considerations for each age group that I typically discuss with my clients in preparation for creating a Life Navigation Plan. Find your phase of life on the worksheet and complete the questions. Then return to the Life Phases Exercise on page 136.

## IN YOUR TWENTIES

☐ I need to start paying down my student loan debt.

☐ I'd like to purchase a new car.

☐ I'd like to purchase or am in the process of purchasing a home. (I would like a fifteen-year mortgage so that I can pay it off by the time I'm forty.)

☐ I have marriage plans.

☐ I have children and want to think about saving for their college educations.

☐ I have a career I'm passionate about.

☐ I want to donate time or money to those in need.

☐ I'd like to give myself permission to have it all!

☐ Other: _____

? Imagine giving yourself permission to have it all. What would your life look like?

_____

_____

_____

_____

# APPENDIX B: LIFE PHASES WORKSHEET

*(continued)*

## IN YOUR THIRTIES

☐ I've sold my first home and bought my second home.

☐ I'm single.

☐ I'm married or partnered.

☐ I have children, and I want to start saving for their college educations.

☐ I've planned my estate and, if I have children, established legal guardianship for my children in case of my death.

☐ I have substantial credit card debt and would like to get it under control.

☐ I'm creating the space in life that I need for myself.

☐ I live a life of financial lack.

☐ I live a life of financial abundance.

☐ I want to change my financial karma.

☐ Other: _____

Imagine changing the things you can in your life and letting go of the things you can't control. List some of those things here.

### THINGS I CAN CHANGE

_____

_____

_____

_____

### THINGS I CAN'T CONTROL

_____

_____

_____

_____

# IN YOUR FORTIES

☐ I'm still passionate about my work.

☐ It's time for me to move on from my current job.

☐ My risk tolerance in regard to my money is at the same level same now as it has been in the past.

☐ My risk tolerance in regard to my money has changed. It has gone (circle one) up / down.

☐ I'm on the path toward having enough income to work less by the time I'm _____ years old.

☐ I'm on track for complete financial independence by the time I'm _____ years old.

☐ My life still feels fresh and exciting.

☐ I have interests, activities and companions that feed my soul.

☐ Other: _____

Describe the life you have chosen thus far.

_____

_____

_____

_____

_____

_____

# APPENDIX B: LIFE PHASES WORKSHEET

*(continued)*

## IN YOUR FIFTIES

- ☐ I'm responsible for the care of my aging parents.
- ☐ My legal documents, including my will, are up to date.
- ☐ I want to leave a legacy of _____ to my children or other heirs.
- ☐ I'd like to reduce the number of hours I work per week in order to enjoy other aspects of life.
- ☐ My house will be paid off before I turn sixty.
- ☐ I have specific intentions for the money that used to go toward my mortgage.
- ☐ I'll be finished paying for my children's college expenses before I turn sixty.
- ☐ I have specific intentions for the money that used to go toward college expenses.
- ☐ I need to plan for long-term care.
- ☐ I would like to start a new career.
- ☐ Other: _____

How do you want to define your life from this point forward?

_____

_____

_____

_____

_____

_____

# IN YOUR SIXTIES

☐ I'm still caring for aging parents.

☐ My legal documents, including my will, are up to date.

☐ I want to leave a legacy of _____ to my children or other heirs.

☐ I'm already retired.

☐ I plan to retire in the near future.

☐ If I retire, my income will decrease substantially.

☐ I plan to work as long as I can.

☐ I have specific plans for retirement.

☐ My house will be paid off before I turn seventy.

☐ I have specific intentions for the money that used to go toward my mortgage.

☐ I'll be finished paying for my children's college expenses before I turn seventy.

☐ I have specific intentions for the money that used to go toward college expenses.

☐ I need to plan for long-term care.

☐ My investment management strategy still matches my goals now that I'm shifting from my accumulation to my distribution years.

☐ It's important to me that I contribute financially to support my grandchildren's or other young relatives' dreams.

☐ Other: _____

What do you feel is your purpose at this point in your life? Has this purpose changed since you reached age sixty?

_____

_____

_____

_____

_____

# APPENDIX B: LIFE PHASES WORKSHEET

*(continued)*

## IN YOUR SEVENTIES

- ☐ My retirement is playing out as I planned it.
- ☐ I prefer to keep working at least part-time as long as I can.
- ☐ My legal documents, including my will, are up to date.
- ☐ I do not plan to leave an inheritance.
- ☐ I plan to leave an inheritance.
- ☐ I would like to start gifting money to my heirs while I'm still living.
- ☐ My house will be paid off before I turn eighty.
- ☐ I have specific intentions for the money that used to go toward my mortgage.
- ☐ My risk tolerance for investments is currently (circle one) higher than / lower than / the same as it used to be.
- ☐ My investment management strategy still matches my goals now that I'm shifting from my accumulation to my distribution years.
- ☐ I need to plan for long-term care.
- ☐ I continue to find ways to be actively engaged in my personal, financial, work and family life.
- ☐ I feel physically, mentally and emotionally healthy.
- ☐ Other: _____

What regrets would you like to address, and what unmet goals would you still like to accomplish? (I had a client who went to law school in his 70s. Harriet Doerr published her first novel at age 73.)

_____

_____

_____

_____

# IN YOUR EIGHTIES

☐ My retirement is playing out as I planned it.

☐ I prefer to keep working at least part-time as long as I can.

☐ My legal documents, including my will, are up to date.

☐ I do not plan to leave an inheritance.

☐ I plan to leave an inheritance.

☐ I would like to start gifting money to my heirs while I'm still living.

☐ My risk tolerance for investments is currently (circle one) higher than / lower than / the same as it used to be.

☐ I continue to find ways to be actively engaged in my personal, financial, work and family life.

☐ I feel physically, mentally and emotionally healthy.

☐ I have regrets I would like to address and/or unmet goals I still want to accomplish.

☐ Other: _____

**?** What's really important to you in your life from this point forward?

_____

_____

_____

_____

# APPENDIX C:
# SHOPPING FOR A TRUSTED ADVISOR

Complete one of the Financial Services Consultation worksheets on the following pages during your first meeting with a financial services professional. When you have met with several professionals, compare the information you've gathered and make your decision from there. Remember, you want someone who really listens to you and who has the capacity to help you make the plans that will lead to your heart's desires.

Write your answers to the "Questions for the Financial Services Professional" during your consultation. Afterward, take a few minutes to record your impressions of the financial services professional by answering the section called "Questions to Ask Yourself" on the worksheet. Once you have chosen a serious candidate, check that person's references. If you're on the fence about a candidate, checking his or her references might help you make your decision.

# FINANCIAL SERVICES CONSULTATION

Date

Name of Financial Professional

Firm

Contact Information (telephone, e-mail)

References

## QUESTIONS FOR THE FINANCIAL SERVICES PROFESSIONAL

? Is your income ☐ fee-based or ☐ commission-based?

? What designations do you have? (I suggest a Certified Financial Planner or CFP®.)

? Are you tied to any sales goals with specific products? ☐ Yes ☐ No  If yes, which products?

Do you have any quotas you must reach, meaning are you working with any vendors who require you to sell a minimum number of their products or your contract with them will end? ☐ Yes ☐ No  If yes, which vendors?

_____

What are your limitations, if any, in selling specific product lines due to your current licensing? (Someone who is fully licensed has a Series 7 and Series 66 to be fee-based.)

_____

_____

Do you charge an annual planning fee outside of compensation from products? ☐ Yes ☐ No  If no, why not?

_____

_____

(If you're talking to an independent planner) If something were to happen to you, who would take care of my interests?

_____

(If you're talking to someone associated with a firm) What happens if you leave the business by choice, disability or death? Who would then be managing my money?

_____

# NOTES

Date _____

Name of Financial Professional _____

## QUESTIONS TO ASK YOURSELF

Did the financial services professional

☐ answer your questions in a thoughtful and thorough way?

☐ ask meaningful questions?

☐ listen carefully?

☐ treat you like an individual?

☐ speak a language you could understand, or at least translate well?

☐ display a capacity for understanding your emotion behind money?

☐ display the mindset and flexibility to shift your funds to your best advantage as your dreams and goals change?

Which of the following qualities does this person display?

☐ Empathy

☐ Passion

☐ Conviction

☐ Tough love

☐ Clarity

## NOTES

_____

_____

_____

_____

_____

# FINANCIAL SERVICES CONSULTATION

Date

Name of Financial Professional

Firm

Contact Information (telephone, e-mail)


References



## QUESTIONS FOR THE FINANCIAL SERVICES PROFESSIONAL

? Is your income ☐ fee-based or ☐ commission-based?


? What designations do you have? (I suggest a Certified Financial Planner or CFP®.)


? Are you tied to any sales goals with specific products? ☐ Yes ☐ No
If yes, which products?

Do you have any quotas you must reach, meaning are you working with any vendors who require you to sell a minimum number of their products or your contract with them will end? ☐ Yes ☐ No  If yes, which vendors?

_____

What are your limitations, if any, in selling specific product lines due to your current licensing? (Someone who is fully licensed has a Series 7 and Series 66 to be fee-based.)

_____

_____

Do you charge an annual planning fee outside of compensation from products? ☐ Yes ☐ No  If no, why not?

_____

_____

(If you're talking to an independent planner) If something were to happen to you, who would take care of my interests?

_____

(If you're talking to someone associated with a firm) What happens if you leave the business by choice, disability or death? Who would then be managing my money?

_____

# NOTES

Date

Name of Financial Professional

## QUESTIONS TO ASK YOURSELF

Did the financial services professional

- ☐ answer your questions in a thoughtful and thorough way?
- ☐ ask meaningful questions?
- ☐ listen carefully?
- ☐ treat you like an individual?
- ☐ speak a language you could understand, or at least translate well?
- ☐ display a capacity for understanding your emotion behind money?
- ☐ display the mindset and flexibility to shift your funds to your best advantage as your dreams and goals change?

Which of the following qualities does this person display?

- ☐ Empathy
- ☐ Passion
- ☐ Conviction
- ☐ Tough love
- ☐ Clarity

## NOTES

# FINANCIAL SERVICES CONSULTATION

Date _____

Name of Financial Professional _____

Firm _____

Contact Information (telephone, e-mail) _____

_____

References _____

_____

_____

## QUESTIONS FOR THE FINANCIAL SERVICES PROFESSIONAL

Is your income ☐ fee-based or ☐ commission-based?

_____

What designations do you have? (I suggest a Certified Financial Planner or CFP®.)

_____

Are you tied to any sales goals with specific products? ☐ Yes ☐ No
If yes, which products?

_____

Do you have any quotas you must reach, meaning are you working with any vendors who require you to sell a minimum number of their products or your contract with them will end? ☐ Yes ☐ No  If yes, which vendors?

_____

What are your limitations, if any, in selling specific product lines due to your current licensing? (Someone who is fully licensed has a Series 7 and Series 66 to be fee-based.)

_____

_____

Do you charge an annual planning fee outside of compensation from products? ☐ Yes ☐ No  If no, why not?

_____

_____

(If you're talking to an independent planner) If something were to happen to you, who would take care of my interests?

_____

(If you're talking to someone associated with a firm) What happens if you leave the business by choice, disability or death? Who would then be managing my money?

_____

# NOTES

Date _____

Name of Financial Professional _____

## QUESTIONS TO ASK YOURSELF

? Did the financial services professional
- ☐ answer your questions in a thoughtful and thorough way?
- ☐ ask meaningful questions?
- ☐ listen carefully?
- ☐ treat you like an individual?
- ☐ speak a language you could understand, or at least translate well?
- ☐ display a capacity for understanding your emotion behind money?
- ☐ display the mindset and flexibility to shift your funds to your best advantage as your dreams and goals change?

? Which of the following qualities does this person display?
- ☐ Empathy
- ☐ Passion
- ☐ Conviction
- ☐ Tough love
- ☐ Clarity

## NOTES

_____

_____

_____

_____

_____

CPSIA information can be obtained
at www.ICGtesting.com
Printed in the USA
BVHW022202290623
666603BV00007B/382

9 780578 837628